W9-BXV-841

beautiful scars

A Life Redefined

beautiful scars

A Life Redefined

Kilee Brookbank + Lori Highlander

with Jessica Noll

Text copyright © 2017 KiCam Projects
All rights reserved.

Unless otherwise indicated, all photos are copyright Kilee Brookbank and
Lori Highlander.

Published by KiCam Projects
109 N. Main St.
Georgetown, OH 45121
KiCamProjects.com

ISBN (paperback): 978-0-9985216-3-3
e-ISBN 978-0-9985216-5-7

Cover design by Mark Sullivan
Cover photography by Emmy Jenkins

Printed in the United States of America

This book is dedicated to the people who save lives, especially those at Shriners Hospitals for Children—Cincinnati: the doctors, nurses, and volunteers who make it such a special place.

This book is also dedicated to everyone going through life-changing setbacks or challenges.

There is hope.

You can heal.

Contents

CHAPTER ONE

Change

Kilee:

The whole thing happened so fast that it didn't seem real.

I walked past the bathroom and got a whiff of the odor again. It was terrible—really terrible. It was nasty, and I didn't want to sit in the house with it smelling like that. It was gross.

The smell had permeated the living room. It was about 4:20 PM, and after a half hour of that stench, I'd had enough.

I walked into the kitchen and slid open the drawer, fumbling around until I found a lighter. I was on a mission. I glanced over to see that the dogs were on the couch as I walked into the bathroom and snatched the cinnamon mocha-scented candle.

It was almost out of wax because we had used it so often. It was so low that I had to stick my entire hand inside the glass jar, meeting the top of the wick with the lighter. With a steady thumb, I rolled down the silver spark wheel and pushed down the red button on the lighter, igniting a small flame on the candlewick. Click.

BOOM!

A flash of overwhelming heat hit me. I was enveloped by raging flames.

It was intensely hot on my face.

The scorching flash blasted my face and blew me to the ground without warning. It didn't feel like I was burning. It felt like when you open the oven door and the heat hits your face. It didn't hurt. It was just hot.

I flew backward and hit my head on the toilet.

I woke up, confused, to the sound of my dog, Digger, barking at me. Just a few minutes before, it seemed, I had been thinking about taking a nap; at first I thought maybe it was all a dream.

Is this really happening?

When I realized it wasn't a dream, my instincts told me to run.

Run fast.

I stumbled outside and looked around. Digger was still with me, but I was disoriented. I wasn't sure what was happening or if any of it was real.

My head was throbbing, and I was hot—super hot. The next realization was a second violent blast: I was on fire.

My life changed on November 10, 2014.

It's what I've done with that moment, and every moment after, that defines me today. Nothing was going to kill my spirit. Back then, I was a normal sixteen-year-old girl. We live in Georgetown, in rural Ohio. There are just under five thousand people in Georgetown. Most have lived there their entire lives, many for generations. Everyone knows everyone else and news travels fast. My days were typical for a teenager in small-town America. I worried about my friends and school. I was always caught up in the drama at school and sometimes at home. But things changed for me in the blink of an eye. Over the next year, I struggled to become myself again. In the process, I realized that I'm not the person I once was—or thought I was. I'm stronger.

I learned that my journey was about understanding myself and not worrying about things that don't matter. Now, no matter how bad my day is, I look at my beautiful scars and know it's never really that bad. Not only did I survive, but I live my life better than ever, helping others and making life worth living every single day.

After that day, nothing has ever been the same for me and for those around me. But I came to understand that might be OK.

Monday Blues

My day started like any other grueling Monday, getting up way too early and dragging myself out of my comfortable, warm bed to get ready for school.

I was sixteen and definitely not a morning person.

Begrudgingly, I woke up at 6:30, but I still didn't get up and get ready. My mom made me get out of bed about ten minutes later. I went to the bathroom and brushed my teeth and then went back to my room, lay down, and went back to sleep.

I woke up on my own about fifteen minutes later.

After picking out my clothes—a chore that took forever because I never knew what I wanted to wear—I got dressed. I wore my teal blue sparkly "Talk DECA to me" T-shirt (DECA is a school club for students and professionals in finance and marketing), black leggings, and black Uggs. Then I wrapped around my wrist a brown leather bracelet with "KILEE" embroidered on it.

I straightened my long chestnut hair, whipped it up into a ponytail, and slid a headband over my forehead, pushing my bangs back out of my face. I applied some light makeup.

Lacking any enthusiasm, I slid into my red Corolla and started the fifteen-mile trek to Ripley-Union-Lewis-Huntington High School in Ripley, Ohio. I dreaded going inside. I sat in my car until the very last minute.

My first class was Spanish. Mondays are never great, but this made it awful. And wouldn't you know it? I sat down only to hear, "You have a test on vocabulary words..." A what?

It got ugly. Everyone thought the test was unfair, and my teacher thought no one was prepared. It seemed like the worst test ever. I wrote down maybe one word and then even tried to copy off the person next to me, who didn't know the words either. I told my teacher, "I don't know what you want me to do about it, but here it is. I'm not finishing it, because I can't finish it. I just don't understand the words you're saying." I sat back down.

I was so mad that I started crying, which is very unlike me. I left all my stuff and rushed to the bathroom. After I cooled off for a minute, I walked back to the classroom and threw my stuff into my book bag.

At this point, a concerned teacher had already asked me if I was OK. When I finally went back to my classroom, five girlfriends and some of my guy friends were making sure I was OK. I told them I was fine; I just didn't want to talk to anyone. As soon as the bell rang, I stormed out.

The rest of the day I was just mad. Really, really mad.

My last class of the day was one of the few things I liked about school. It was my pottery class.

Pottery was the best, because I could use my creativity to make whatever I wanted. The previous week I had created a mug, and it was finally finished firing in the kiln. I loved painting my pottery because I could finally make it look the way I wanted.

I chose pretty shades of pink, blue, and purple. With a paintbrush in my hand, I swiped the mug, making it beautiful, one stroke at a time. By the end of the class, my hands were covered in brightly colored paint, but I didn't care. I loved my mug.

Homebound

It wasn't too long after the end of soccer season, and I was just getting used to not having practice or games after school. I could just go home and do homework or sit on the couch and watch TV. And that's what I was going to do—especially after the day I'd had.

But first, food!

On my way home, I decided to stop at McDonald's, because lunch hadn't been great. I thought school lunches were gross, so I'd only had a bag of Doritos and a Gatorade. I hit the drive-thru and ordered a plain McChicken, medium fries, and a large Sprite.

I got home at 3:45 PM. As soon as I walked in, I smelled something strange...like poop. I saw food containers from the previous night's dinner and figured my stepbrother had come home, eaten, and done something to stink up the bathroom.

I kicked off my boots and headed to the bathroom; the smell was definitely stronger in there. We keep our dogs, Doogie and Digger, in the bathroom during the day. They are tiny Chihuahua-Yorkshire terrier mixes and can really do a lot of damage if left to roam the house alone. I let them outside and packed up my phone charger and shoes while waiting for my brother, Cameron, to get done with basketball practice. We were leaving at six to go to our dad's house for the week.

Not long before four o'clock, my mom called me and we talked briefly. I asked her where Cameron was—normally, he would have been home already. She told me he was staying at school until basketball practice, and I told her I would pick him up on my way to our dad's house later that evening.

She told me she would be home at 4:30. I said, "OK. I love you," and hung up.

I got off the couch to let the dogs back in, but when I walked past the bathroom, the smell was even stronger.

Ignoring it, I started texting with my friend. My thumbs could type hundreds of letters a second, I'm sure. I was complaining to him about my bum phone. Again.

The iPhone 6 had just come out. Excited to be able to get one, I'd ordered it four weeks earlier, but I hadn't known it was going to take a month to get to me. I was mad.

When it had finally arrived, I started opening the package and heard a noise from inside the box. I opened it up and the screen was popped off the phone. I had waited so long for it! Now I'd have to send it back and wait some more. Ugh!

I could tell my text-ranting about the phone was annoying my friend. I was complaining. A lot.

I texted him, "I still can't believe that…"

"Yeah, me either, but it doesn't matter," he texted back.

"Yes it does. I waited so long for it and that's what they give me?"

"It'll be OK."

I just kept going on and on about it.

Finally, he texted, "There are more important things to worry about."

Lori:

My morning was like any other. I got the kids up at 6:30, and since Kilee struggles in the morning, I had to go in and wake her up again…and again. I sat her up on the bed and she slowly woke up every time. I drove Cameron to school, and Kilee waited for me, as always, to get back. She knew I liked saying good-bye and "I love you" every morning before she left.

I then headed to the office, which was in town and just five minutes from the house. I spend most of my time managing programs that help adults in addiction and recovery. I had a meeting at eleven with our clinical director. We talked about work, but also on a personal level about Cameron and sports. My son always strives to be better. Our clinical director referees games, and he was talking to me about how Cameron was big for thirteen and seemed to have great potential. We had lunch together and he left the office around 2:30.

Cameron had texted me, asking if his friend could go to the house with him. I said, "I don't care, buddy."

"OK, I'll text you and let you know what we're doing for sure."

He texted me back about a half hour later and said they were just going to stay at school for practice.

"All right, buddy, that's fine. Just text me when you walk over to the gym."

His practice was at the elementary school, which is behind the junior-senior high school. I knew he was safe and with his friends. I told him to make use of his time and do his homework.

I went to the house, and as I walked inside, I noticed my stepson Houstin's leftovers on the counter and thought, *I'm not cleaning that up right now.*

I would have let the dogs out, but I was in a hurry.

They were whining at the door for me, so I yelled to them, "Boys, I'll be home in an hour!"

I needed to bring Cameron's basketball clothes to him at school. I walked straight to his room, grabbed his stuff, and walked out the back door. I dropped off the clothes at school and went back to the office.

Kilee called me.

She called every day after school to let me know she'd gotten home all right. We talked about everyday stuff. She never mentioned anything about having a bad day—bombing the Spanish test—but she did say something about her phone arriving broken. She was frustrated. She told me she didn't have much homework.

We talked about plans for that week. Since soccer had ended two weeks earlier, she had more free time.

I told her I'd be home around 4:30 to help her get ready to go to her dad's house. She had a very neat and pretty room and always liked to make sure everything was picked up and in order before she left. So I would often help her with that.

Before hanging up, I told her, "I love you."

"I love you, too, Mom."

My sister, Amy, is my coworker. She is also my best friend. As she came into my office, I remember noticing the time: 3:53. We talked for a while about her daughter, Loren, and Kilee and their friendship.

Kilee and Loren are cousins and best friends. They'd hit a rough patch. Kilee is hardheaded and Loren is tenderhearted. But they were starting to get close again.

Squealing sirens interrupted us.

Like a Dream

Kilee:

Stumbling outside to the back deck, shuffling through shattered glass and splintered doors, I walked—my feet bare except for what was left of my burned socks—across the lawn, thirty feet to the steps of my neighbors' back porch.

Our longtime neighbors, Carol and Stanley, had rushed outside to meet me. I was standing on their porch screaming.

"Help! Help!"

I didn't know what was going on, but I knew something wasn't right.

Carol ran inside. She came back out with a bowl of water and dumped it over my head. As the water drained down my face and sizzled on contact, I said, "Thank you," but kept yelling out of sheer and utter fear. "Get this off! Help me! Please help me! Oh, God, please help me!"

Stanley ripped off my sparkly shirt and started vigorously patting my body, scorching his own hands.

It was hot, but it didn't really hurt.

Another neighbor, an off-duty police officer, came running over. As he and Stanley helped me, Stanley told Carol to call 911. My house was still on fire, and I tried to look at it, but they wouldn't let me. Our house was going up in flames, along with all our personal belongings and all our memories.

I knew then that something was really, really wrong.

"Her hands! They're melting off of her!"

I could hear Carol telling the 911 dispatch operator that they had me, but that the house was still on fire.

She was belting: "This is an emergency. I need someone at 312 Free Soil Road. A little girl is on fire back here!…312 Free Soil, she's burning…something blew up… . I don't know— 14, 15, 16, I think. Could you hurry? She's still burning!…The house is on fire too—could you call the fire department?… The little girl is still burning! Her hands! They're melting off of her!…We put water on her. I think we've got the fire out, but now she's hysterical… Her hair was on fire. Her stomach was burning. Her hands are burnt. I still smell her…I need to call her mother and father."

It was all too surreal. I turned around to see the fire billowing out of the bathroom window.

"Put this around her to keep her warm," Carol told Stanley. Then, to both Stanley and the 911 operator: "That whole house is on fire. It's gonna blow!"

After hanging up with 911, Carol called my mom, who was at work just minutes up the road.

Leaving a trail of water and soot, Stanley helped me to the blacktopped driveway. It was cold. There was nothing on my butt—my pants had burned off. People driving by were stopping, parking in the road, and getting out of their cars, asking what happened and if I was going to be OK.

One of the bystanders who had stopped knew my stepdad, Wade, pretty well and called him. Wade was the first one to show up.

Once he spotted me on the driveway, he ran over and told me everything was going to be OK, and then he gave me his sweatshirt. I was freezing.

While I appreciated everything he was trying to do, I knew everything was not OK.

The ambulance arrived about five minutes later.

I could hear other sirens in the distance, getting louder and louder as they got closer. Everything around me was blurry and seemed like a dream again.

༄ ༄

Lori:

At 4:18, Amy and I started to hear sirens, getting louder and louder, until they were screeching past the office. I looked out my window—the holiday lights were already on Main Street's light poles for Christmas.

Amy said, "You hear those sirens?"

"Yeah, that's the third one that's gone by."

"I'd better text Loren and find out where she is; she's not home yet," Amy said, and she left for her office.

Fire trucks kept flying past the office and I thought, something's not right. Something bad is going on. I didn't think to call Kilee, though, because I had just talked to her and knew she was safe at home.

Amy walked back into my office and said, "Well, it's not Loren; she's fine."

Relieved, I noticed my phone was ringing as Amy returned to her office. Wade was calling me.

I had just talked to him a few minutes before, so I answered with attitude, "Yeah?"

He said, "Lori, our house is on fire!"

He didn't know Kilee was at home.

"What?"

"Our house is on fire!"

"You've got to be kidding me!"

"No! Meet me at home!"

And we hung up.

But I still knew Kilee was safe. *I knew it.* I had just talked to her. She was safe. My mind wouldn't let me think anything else.

I jumped up and ran into Amy's office and said, "Amy! My house is on fire!"

I ran out, but forgot my keys and had to turn around. I ran back in, grabbed my keys, and, as I was running around, I was trying to call Kilee.

I said, "Amy! The dogs are in the house!" As soon as it came out of my mouth, I said, "Oh my gosh…Kilee's in the house."

Everything just stopped.

I ran out of the office, got into my car, and started driving home. I didn't have any idea what I was driving home to.

I kept calling Kilee, and her phone kept ringing and ringing. That seemed odd, but I thought it couldn't be that bad if her phone is still ringing. Usually if a phone is done, it goes straight to voicemail. So I'm thinking, she's got to be OK; she's got to be safe, because the phone is ringing.

After my second attempt to call Kilee, my neighbor Carol called, interrupting my third call.

She said, "Lori…"

"Yes, our house is on fire!"

"Yeah, I know. I've got Kilee," she said.

"Oh my gosh!"

"She's OK."

I said, "OK, OK, OK."

I was still nervous. I was crying and hysterical and upset, but I was thinking, *All right, she's OK. She's alive and she's OK.* I didn't think she was hurt. I only kept thinking, *She's OK. If it were really bad and the house had burned down, Kilee's phone would have gone straight to voicemail.*

I think I got there in a minute flat. I pulled in—rather, I ramped my car into the lot beside our house. Somehow, people were already everywhere…but it had just happened. We'd heard the sirens go by only a few minutes ago.

Fire was coming out of Kilee's windows. It was bad, so bad. It was gushing out of her windows and I wondered, *Did she come out of her room? Was she still in her room?* I knew she would have been packing for the week at her dad's house.

The fire chief tried to guide me away from the house because the windows were blown out and there was glass everywhere. I was just looking for Kilee.

"Where is she?"

He pointed me toward her.

I was frantic. I was going nuts. I saw that window, with all of those flames, and I just kept thinking, *She must have been in there. How is she even alive?*

I ran across to Carol and Stanley's driveway. Kilee was facing away from our house, her back toward me as I sprinted to her. She was sitting on the blacktop.

I started screaming, "Oh my gosh! Kilee! Kilee!"

She looked at me and said, "Mom, you have to calm down. If you don't stop freaking out, I'm going to start freaking out."

Amy was right behind me. Crying, I hugged Kilee. Amy tried, but Kilee said, "No, no, no. That doesn't feel good."

The first thing I noticed when I saw her was her hair.

It was already a little shorter than usual because she had just gotten it cut off the month before. Her hair had always been long, cascading halfway down her back. She texted me after getting it cut and said, "It's OK." She was looking forward to letting it grow back out.

Now, her hair was completely singed. If you've ever had a beautician chemically burn your hair, or seen the fried, wire-like strands of hair from excessive blow-drying and straightening, it looked like that, but ten times worse. It was burnt all the way up. It was still long, but four inches were gone.

I looked at her hair and thought, *It's OK. We can work with it. It's just short; we'll cut it and fix it. She'll just have to grow it back out.* It was before I knew the extent of her injuries.

She looked up at me and asked: "How are my eyelashes? How are my eyebrows? How's my hair?"

I lied.

It was weird. It was like she had gone to the salon and had her eyebrows perfectly shaped, yet they were gone. Her doe-like eyelashes also were gone—barely any stubble.

She'd always had really poor vision in one lazy eye. Now I saw that her other eye—the good one—had a black piece of metal in it.

She had scuffs and scratches all over her face, but she wasn't bleeding.

I told myself, *She's fine. She's fine. She doesn't look that bad.*

Wade was sitting in front of her. She was freezing and had coats wrapped around her. She had ripped her shirt off. All she had on was her bra, leggings that had splotchy burn holes throughout, and socks with barely anything left to them.

She said, "Wade, hold me. I'm cold."

Wade tried to cuddle her, but she said, "Be careful."

She told me she felt normal, kind of numb. But her hands felt a little different.

Looking down at Kilee's fingers and feet, peeping out from the coat draped over her, I just tried focusing on her sparkly pink fingernail polish and her aqua toenail polish.

It's going to be OK. It's not as bad as we think—I can see her nail polish.

She was going to be OK. She had to be.

CHAPTER TWO

A Smile Is Born

Kilee:

My life growing up was the best a little girl could ask for. I was loved by all four of my parents and step-parents, and I always felt loved wherever I was. My brother and I grew up very close, just like the rest of our family. My favorite part of each day was when I could spend time with my family. Family is everything.

Lori:

Kilee's dad, Jason, has always called Kilee "Smiley Kilee." And for good reason.

Kilee has smiled from ear to ear from the moment she was born. She was a very happy little girl—and smart, funny, energetic, and completely adorable.

She's loving toward me, her dad, Cameron (when she wants to be), Amy, and Loren. That's it. That is her safe zone. She's pretty private. But she's always been polite. I've been complimented on how polite she is; it's always "thank you" and "please."

More Than Skin Deep

Kilee has always been beautiful, just beautiful. Perfect. Her skin, hair…she's the girl in school you're jealous of. And she's modest, which makes it worse. She doesn't flaunt anything. She is who she is and that is it.

I feel the same when I look at her now as when she was born: She's just perfect.

It's easy for people to get blinded by what happened to her and see only scars. But I don't look at her and see scars. I look at her and see perfect Kilee. I view her scars as the reason she's alive. If she didn't have scars, she wouldn't be here, alive, today.

When this happened to her, everyone worried about how she would feel about having scars and people staring at or bullying her.

I didn't even think about that, ever. I didn't think about it, personality-wise, whether she was going to be able to deal with this. She's strong and hardheaded. If she gets something in her mind, she's going to do it.

Kids or No Kids?

I never knew I wanted kids…until I did.

Although I came from a highly educated household, the dysfunction surrounding me made me second-guess having children of my own one day.

Jason and I had been together for five years before we got married. It's funny, because in high school I always said that I wasn't going to have kids. I didn't think I wanted them.

I graduated and went to college. I commuted because I was on my own and I had to work. My first year, I just wanted to hang out with my friends, but I had two jobs and was going to school full-time. I didn't know how I was going to juggle everything and still do what I wanted. It wasn't how I planned it, but I was on my own and I paid for everything myself. I had a scholarship that helped, but I had to pay for room and board and my books.

Through one of my jobs, I met a good friend. He and his wife had three kids at the time, all under the age of three. We were close because we worked a lot of evenings and weekends together at a drug and alcohol residential treatment center.

One day, he told me that his wife was pregnant with their fourth child. He was excited about it, but she was overwhelmed.

I was there for them the whole time, and finally, baby girl Quincey was born. I babysat her for the first time when she was a week old. Her parents were overwhelmed with four young kids. I could only imagine how hard that was for them. My friend worked two jobs, and his wife was working on her Ph.D. They were incredibly busy. I didn't know how I could fit it in with my own jobs and classes, but I wanted to help.

I kept Quincey frequently. Jason would help, and we both enjoyed watching her. But it was hard separating from her and giving her back to her parents after having her for so long.

After about a year of watching her, I realized I wanted kids.

Amy was pregnant with Loren, and I was about to get married. I thought maybe we should start having kids immediately. So we did.

I was twenty-one when Jason and I built a new house and got married. I graduated from college, and we got pregnant within a month of being married.

I really think that Loren and Quincey made me realize how much I truly did want a child, even though months prior I would've sworn I didn't. But I am grateful to this day that that happened to me.

The Greatest Love

I wanted a girl. That quickly changed to wanting a healthy baby.

The doctor who had delivered me and my sister and was caring for me during my pregnancy called me on the phone after I'd had a 3-D ultrasound. I had several complications. I was high-risk, and my baby was breech. And they said there was a lump in the back of my baby's neck.

Of course, at thirty-seven weeks pregnant, you're overwhelmed to begin with; you're huge and you can't breathe and you have all these medical problems. I was still working full-time, and I tried to stay calm. I didn't think of the worst or what I would do. I just knew that this was my baby and it was going to be OK. I accepted that, even though she was on my mind every day, all day long.

It was my baby. I didn't care. Whatever I'm dealt, I'll handle it, I thought.

I watched as my brother's son was born with Goldenhar syndrome. No one had any idea anything was wrong with him. My brother and sister-in-law were told he was going to be a nine-pound baby; instead, he was born only four pounds, and the whole right side of his face was malformed. He was deaf and had many other health problems. He was in a children's hospital for quite a while before he could even go home.

My brother and sister-in-law handled it well. They didn't know this was going to happen to their baby, but they figured it out and dealt with it. My brother accepted his son 100 percent; nothing else mattered, because that boy was his child.

I think that experience prepared Jason and me to deal with the uncertainty we faced. I thought, *If my baby has Down syndrome, that's OK. At least it's not all of the other health issues my nephew went through and continues to go through.*

I switched doctors because I didn't like the way I was treated when they called me on the phone to tell me about Kilee's possible complications. I think you deal with situations better—and worry less—with education, explanation, and preparation; all we received was a phone call telling us our lives could be changed forever and our baby could have problems. It was like hearing, "Here's your baby. Figure it out."

After I switched, my new doctor told me about even more complications I hadn't known about. Then they put me on bed rest at thirty-eight weeks.

I was twenty-two years old, and my little baby came eleven days early on Tuesday, June 2, 1998, 12:58 PM. It was a beautiful summer day and the perfect day to meet my baby.

The birth wasn't quite so perfect. They had to do an emergency C-section because my blood pressure was too high.

I went in not knowing the sex of the baby. I wanted it to be a surprise. But I had a feeling. I just knew I was going to have a little girl.

"Greatest Love of All" by Whitney Houston was playing as they pulled that tiny body out of me. You don't think a song will affect you, but it does. I'll never forget it.

When she was born, I kept staring into her eyes. I kept looking at her, thinking, *She's perfect.*

And Kilee was perfect.

She weighed eight pounds, eight-and-a-half ounces and was twenty-one inches long. She was the prettiest baby I had ever seen.

It was the most wonderful feeling ever. There's nothing else that can beat that feeling. I was happy. Jason was happy. We just couldn't believe it.

Growing Up Kilee

Kilee has always been happy and smiley, except when she had colic for a few weeks, but other than that, she was very healthy.

I had saved up some money so I could take three months off work to stay home with her. I also wanted to find something new professionally.

I interviewed for new jobs during that time and accepted an offer as a junior accountant. The night before I was supposed to start, I called and told them I couldn't leave my child. She was three months old by then, but Kilee was stuck with me.

I started working with my mom at a drug and alcohol treatment center and I took Kilee to work with me all the time.

Kilee was a happy baby. And she's happy yet shy today. She was always on my hip or Jason's hip, always right by our side.

She was advanced, always doing things sooner than the development charts predicted. She talked at six months, walked at eleven months.

She knew her address, telephone number, and her ABCs before she went to preschool. She was already ahead. I credit that to me being able to bring her to work and spend so much one-on-one time with her. When you're there for your kids and work with them and read books to them every night, it makes a big difference in their progress and how they develop and learn.

Kilee was an outside kid, even when it was cold. It didn't matter if there was snow on the ground, she was outside. But she did not like dirt. If she got dirt on her hands from playing outside, she would march straight inside and have me help her wash her hands.

When she was eight, Kilee thought she wanted to be a cheerleader. Because of her shyness, I had my doubts. Sure enough, after she got out in front of everyone, she said, "Mom, I don't like this…"

She finished the season and never cheered again. She has been the same kid since the day she was born.

The Lessons of Childhood

So many people say you have a different bond with a girl than you do a boy. And to a certain extent, I think you could and people do, but I love both of my kids unconditionally and the same way.

If they need something, I'm there for them. If they do something wrong, I'm there for them—but they're going to face consequences. I've learned a lot about how to raise my kids from the way I was raised, by seeing what not to do.

Growing up, we were comfortable financially, but our family was dysfunctional. People assume that if you make a nice living, you live a perfect life, but that's just not the way it was.

My parents are educated. My dad has a teaching degree; he's a Vietnam veteran who lost his legs in the war. My mom is a master's-level licensed chemical dependency counselor, with several other accompanying licenses. Despite all of this education and experience, dysfunction can take over a family. I didn't want that life for my kids, ever.

It's why Jason and I divorced. You can either continue your parents' cycle and live in an unhappy, unhealthy marriage, or you can remove the dysfunction from the household and go your separate ways.

For better or worse, children of divorce become accustomed to change—changes in family life, homes, people, lifestyles. It's not something any parent anticipates or wishes for. That said, maybe a life of change has helped Kilee deal with the changes she has gone through since the explosion, plus the changes that await her in the rest of her life.

Kilee:

I remember my parents fought often before they decided to get a divorce. I didn't really know what was happening.

They were in the kitchen talking one night, and Cameron and I were in his room. He was hungry, so instead of him going out there, I told him to stay in his room while I got him something. I went to the kitchen and made a hot dog for him.

The next day my grandma came over. Cameron and I were confused. I figured that maybe Mom and Dad weren't together anymore. I knew something was up.

My mom has always been a strong person. She's always done everything for my brother and me. When my mom and dad got divorced, I could tell my mom was being strong for Cameron and me.

Back then, my mom and I were never super close. Now, though, I would say my mom and I are very close. I tell her everything. We know each other well. She is still the strong person I remember from when I was growing up, but now she's even stronger.

Blended Families

It has always felt like I have both parents at both houses, my mom and Wade and my dad and Brooke. Not many kids have that. When your family is divorced, normally, you have a mom there and a dad there. But I felt like I had both no matter which house I was staying at.

Though, at first, it was weird.

When Wade and my mom introduced Cameron and me to Wade's kids, Houstin and Collin, we were friends from the beginning. I always felt like they were my brothers. We had stuff in common. We played outside together, tossed the football. It was cool, because they were like friends you got to see every other week and you got to live with them.

I met Brooke about four years ago. She was young, only twenty-five. She was really shy but really sweet. She didn't say a lot, but she and my dad hit it off. She started coming around more and moved in. It moved pretty fast. They had planned to get married, but then November 10 happened. And they put their plans on hold…that is, until "Smiley Kilee" was back and ready to stand up with her dad on his big day.

Lori:

Seeing Kilee's beautiful smile is infectious and evaporates any fear I have—always has. However, after the explosion, Kilee's smile was wiped from her face and replaced with fear, anger, and frustration. I knew we'd see her smile again, but we'd have to wait a while and she'd have to shed a few tears first.

CHAPTER THREE

Hurting and Healing

Lori:

Our house was black and smoky as firefighters continued to blast water toward the flames and the paramedics pulled onto the scene.

I couldn't believe how calm Kilee was.

The paramedics loaded her up, and before they left, I told her: "You're going to be OK, Kilee. You're going to be OK."

Kilee:

As soon as the paramedics loaded me onto the stretcher, they started peppering me with questions.

"When was the last time you ate? Does anything hurt? Do you feel all right? Can you see OK?"

The medics were acting crazy, frantic. The ambulance started moving, but no one would tell me where I was going. They were trying to put an IV into my neck, but they kept missing, so they had to switch sides. I don't like needles under normal circumstances; all the confusion and panic made everything worse.

But it didn't hurt at all. Nothing hurt. I was confused about why the medics were so busy—poking me with needles, talking to each other with terms I didn't understand. There was nothing wrong. I felt nothing at all.

Then they started cutting away every piece of clothing that was left on me. Now I was really alarmed. How could all this be necessary?

They drove me to the hospital a few minutes away, which had mostly closed down in the past year. There were still a few doctors' offices there and, luckily for me, a place to land a helicopter. My mom met us there. She wanted to go with me in the helicopter. I wanted her to also, but they wouldn't let her because there wasn't enough room. I told her it was OK and I'd be all right.

They loaded me into the helicopter. It was small. Amazingly tiny.

Flying to a Different Life

Lori:

They wouldn't let me ride in the helicopter.

I had calmed down by then. I was still nervous, but I wasn't going to let Kilee see me that freaked out again.

As the paramedics continued to work on Kilee, who by now was stripped down and hooked up to an IV, a woman with the helicopter told me they were taking her to the hospital.

They let me give Kilee a kiss good-bye, and I told her I loved her. I could see in her eyes that she was terrified. I could tell it was bad, but at the time, I didn't know how bad.

The paramedics told me they gave Kilee medication to make her comfortable. Meanwhile, Wade was on the phone, trying to contact people to let them know what was going on. We were getting calls, texts, and emails from everyone, and people from nearby houses were standing outside watching everything unfold.

Before the helicopter took off, the paramedics told me they were going to take Kilee to Cincinnati Children's Hospital, about an hour away. The woman said, "We'll take care of her and get her into the right hands."

While I stood there, I got phone calls and text messages from friends asking if I was OK, if it had been me in the accident. I thought, *How can it get around that fast?* It had been only about fifteen minutes since the explosion happened.

As soon as the helicopter lifted off, I collapsed. I have never felt that way before. I had no control. I couldn't do anything. I just had to sit there and wait to see what would happen next.

I was sick to my stomach. Wade was standing behind me, hugging me, trying to console me.

When we got into the car, he said: "Maybe it isn't as bad as we think it is. Let's not jump to any conclusions until we know. Just calm down."

I said, "OK, but what about her eye?" I was worried about her eye. If her only good eye was damaged…what if she can't see?

I called Jason. He was calm. I couldn't believe how calm he was. In frantic situations, he's not normally the calm one. How could he be calm then? Was it because he hadn't seen what we saw? Hadn't seen Kilee after the explosion?

I told him, "Jason, her hair is gone. It's gone. I mean, it's singed to her head. Her hands don't look very good, but I don't know what that means…it might not be that bad."

My mind began to race. Her hair was singed. Her face was scraped up. Her hands didn't look good. There was something in her eye.

But she didn't look that bad.

She had her wits about her. She wasn't joking or anything; she was scared, but she appeared to be OK. I was trying to tell myself that Kilee was OK. Thinking as clearly as I could, I asked Wade not to speed so we could make it to the hospital safely. So we could be there for her.

Kilee:

I was still on the stretcher, inside the helicopter. They put a mask on my face. They kept asking me questions, asking me if I was all right. I got mad because I just wanted to look out the window, but they would not let me sit up.

They rolled me up into a blanket, kind of like a swaddled baby. I kept trying to look out that window, but they made me stay lying down. The window started to get darker the longer we flew. The sun was going down.

The flight felt like it took forever. When we got to Children's, we landed on the roof and there were a ton of people there to meet us. As they pulled the door open, I could feel that it was cool and breezy outside. The cool air blew on my face once I was out of the helicopter, and it felt good.

I began to realize I couldn't see clearly, that there was something wrong with my left eye.

Everyone started asking me questions I couldn't answer. Again.

"Did you eat in the last hour?"

"I don't know…"

"What happened?"

"I don't know…"

They wheeled my stretcher across the roof to the elevator and got me downstairs. They quickly lifted the sheet I was lying on top of and moved me over to a table. It didn't hurt, but it didn't exactly feel good, either.

There were about twenty doctors and nurses around me. They were checking my eyes, checking every part of my body. They were checking everything. They were asking a million questions, and I tried to answer them the best I could, but the questions seemed so random that I don't know why anyone would need to know.

My dad came into the room. I couldn't reach him.

"Daddy!" I yelled. That wasn't something I usually called him.

When I looked at him, I couldn't see him that well. I asked him if there was something in my eye, and he told me the doctors would get it out. He told me everything was going to be OK. I wasn't so sure with the way the doctors and nurses were rushing around. As they continued to poke and prod me, I screamed, "Daddy, make them stop!"

Once they had some idea about the extent of my injuries (but before I did), they transferred me to Shriners Hospitals for Children–Cincinnati, which specializes in burn care.

Dad rode with me to Shriners in the ambulance, even though it's only like a minute away. Once we got there, they pulled me out from the back of the ambulance. It was really chilly outside. They pushed my stretcher inside Shriners.

That's the last thing I remember from that day.

Lori:

Jason got to Children's Hospital in about forty minutes from Hillsboro, which is usually an hour-and-twenty-minute drive.

When Wade and I got to Children's, Kilee was already being worked on. They finally took me to her while Wade was talking to a friend on the Shriners board of trustees. He was making a call to Shriners to alert them that she was on her way over.

When I saw her, there were dozens of nurses and doctors around her. Everyone was doing something. I just kept thinking, *Why are there so many people in here?* And that is when I saw her hand and arm for the first time.

Oh, God.

It was white, completely white. There was blood around her wrist where she had been wearing a bracelet. It just did not look right. There was something seriously wrong. I knew. I knew right then.

Jason and I decided he would ride in the ambulance with her to Shriners.

I said, "Kilee, are you OK with your dad going with you?"

She was out of it, but she said, "Uh-huh."

I asked one of the nurses where I needed to go. I was so distraught that I forgot how I had gotten to that part of the hospital. I couldn't get out.

I looked around as I was directed back to the waiting area, and Wade was already gone. I looked around, panicking, thinking, *What happened?*

I finally found out that a nurse had told him that I rode over with the ambulance. So he had gone to Shriners, which was next door, to wait. Luckily, Wade's friend from Shriners was still there and told me he would drive me over. He gave me a hug. He understood. His daughter had been burned when she was five years old and has had multiple surgeries—she is in college now.

He told me, "Shriners is the best place for her. You're going to make it. Kilee's going to make it. Everything's going to be all right."

It was comforting. I had heard about their struggles over the years, so it meant a lot to me that he was there.

The First Night

Kilee was already being worked on at Shriners when I got there. They were prepping her and assessing her to determine treatment. She was away from us for three hours. It felt like an eternity. We were just waiting, wondering about the unknown.

It was about seven o'clock when a counselor came to the waiting room to get Jason and me. She took us into an office to talk to us, with a nurse, and to register Kilee into Shriners.

Jason lost it.

At least seventy people showed up at Shriners that night to wait and hear how Kilee was. Friends, family, even the media—the waiting room and the area outside the hospital were full of people. Their love and support made a huge impact on all of us and our recovery as a family, especially getting us through those first few weeks.

Fast forward three hours, and Dr. Richard Kagan came out and told us we needed to talk about Kilee.

Jason, Wade, Brooke, Cameron (who had ridden into town with my sister, Amy), and I were in the room.

I could just feel it that the news was going to be bad.

Dr. Kagan told us she might lose her fingertips or even the mobility of her fingers altogether. That put things into perspective for us. But then he said, "However, we'll know more when we do the surgery and see how bad it really is."

I closed my eyes and gathered myself. Nobody wanted to ask what the chances were that she would survive. But we asked. We had to.

He told us Kilee would be in the ICU for at least a week, possibly longer. And that she had a 95 percent chance of living—a 5 percent chance of a fatal infection because of the severity of her burns and possible complications.

Once he said those words, something calming came over me. I quickly realized there was no better place for her to be.

The counselor and a nurse came in and explained the process: what to do, how to use the CaringBridge website (which is designed to help families navigate medical crises), and basically how things would progress from here—for Kilee and for us.

Jason asked Dr. Kagan what Kilee would be able to do and not be able to do.

The doctor said she would probably be able to do everything that she had been able to do before, with some minor exceptions. It would be based on her progress with therapy, but she'd be able to throw a ball again. When he said that, there was something comforting about it. She might not have fingertips, but she could throw a ball? OK, well, that's good news. He was giving us best- and worst-case scenarios to put everything into perspective.

Dr. Kagan explained to us how he assessed Kilee's burns on her hands and arms, which were third-degree all the way through both layers of the dermis and epidermis and into the fat. There was not much of a protective layer of fat between the skin and the tendons under it. The tendons and joints were in danger with such deep burns—ironically, they tend to hurt less the deeper they are because of possible nerve damage.

Dr. Kagan had to give Kilee IV fluids for resuscitation and wound care on her upper body, where she was swollen and tight from the burns. To prevent long-term damage to the muscles in her arms, the doctor also cut the skin on Kilee's arms, which he told us relieved the pressure and restored blood flow.

We all walked out of there together—hugging, crying, relieved there was a 95 percent chance Kilee would survive. With the counselor, we made an announcement to all of those in the waiting room about Kilee and how she was. Everyone started hugging us. They kept us occupied and prevented our minds from dwelling on what we had no control over. Our friends and family couldn't do anything, but they were there, and that meant everything in that moment. I can never fully repay them, and I hope, for their sakes, that I never have to.

A Miracle Behind Closed Doors

I got to see Kilee around nine o'clock that night. She had started to swell by then. When you have burns like that, you swell really, really badly.

Forty-five percent of her body was burned. About 20 percent of the burns were third-degree and 25 percent were second-degree.

Her arms. Hands. Legs. Buttocks. Back. Feet. Ankles. Belly.

There were little burns all over her face. Kilee's eyelashes were gone, and her eyebrows were nearly gone. The medical team had shaved her head to make sure her scalp wasn't too burned. And she had a feeding tube. Her arms and hands were like porcelain, cold and white. Her eyes were swollen beyond recognition.

She was calling me "Mommy" and Jason "Daddy" and kept telling us over and over how much she loved us.

I made sure I did not cry in there. I did not let her see me cry.

The hardest part was that I couldn't hold her hand. I couldn't hug her, so I touched her head. Her hair had saved her head from burning. There was one little scratch on her head. I just kept rubbing her bald head, kissing the top. It still smelled like fire. It was awful. But I didn't care. It was the only way I could touch Kilee and be there for her.

She was alert and kept apologizing to Wade for his childhood home burning to the ground. She felt bad for him. I told her to stop apologizing. He was bawling and said to her, "Kilee, you're here. That's all that matters to me."

She told us everything that happened at the house. I was floored that she remembered, considering how heavily sedated she was. Kilee told me, "Digger stayed with me, Mom."

She knew at that point that Digger had saved her life.

As she was talking, I was still trying to comprehend everything. Why was there a sewer smell in our house? I had just been there. I didn't smell anything. I was there an hour before and smelled nothing. It just didn't make sense. Houstin, my stepson, was there an hour before me and smelled nothing. It just did not make sense how something like that could have happened. But just to see Kilee and know she was alive meant the world to all of us. We knew there was hope and that she was going to make it through.

That first night, I didn't sleep at all. We stayed in the family suites at Shriners. Wade and I lay there together in a twin bed. I sobbed all night.

We got up early the next morning. The staff had told us that if anything happened throughout the night, if Kilee needed us, they would come to our room. It was comforting to know they would come get us if something happened. The suites were a three-minute walk from Kilee's room.

Rebuilding Life Away from the Hospital

That next day, Kilee was sedated. It was indescribable. But it was best that she was out; we needed to take care of everything else going on.

There wasn't just one thing to worry about. For Wade and me, it was hard because we knew we had our other kids, Cameron and Houstin, to take care of as well, and we couldn't be there for them the way we should be.

Cameron was, of course, a mess. He tried to be strong on the outside, but I knew he wasn't taking it well.

We also kept thinking, *We don't have a house. We need to get all of this stuff in order. We have no belongings.* You don't dwell on losing that stuff, but you realize you have to get it together. There was so much that needed to be done.

Doogie, our other dog, was MIA until late that night. We needed to figure out who was going to watch both dogs. The power was out at the house. Kilee's car was still at the house—it was burned in the front because of how she had parked. Someone needed to go and get her car.

Seemingly unimportant, the tasks were a nuisance, but we knew we had to do them. The whole situation was difficult, and we didn't want to let Kilee know about any of the outside stuff. We wanted her to focus on healing. It was a good feeling to know Kilee was being taken care of and we could make these calls from the hospital. The bad feeling was knowing we had so much further to go on this journey. The end was nowhere in sight. It wasn't going to be over once Kilee healed in Shriners. There was more to it.

The next day, Wednesday, we had to go to the house. It was cold. That Monday had been 65 degrees; by Wednesday, it was 35.

The insurance adjuster said, "I can tell you right now, your house is a complete loss."

We saw it. We went in. We had no doubt he was right.

My first reaction was I couldn't believe Kilee had made it out of that house. I was floored. The house was completely burned. There was nothing left—other than her room, which was odd.

Cameron and I walked through the house. All the walls were black.

Wade went inside, maybe for a minute, and turned around and walked out. He wouldn't stay. He never stepped foot back inside the house he grew up in—his mother had lived there until she passed away just a few years before.

There was nothing left to Cameron's room. Wade's and my room, as well as Houstin's room, was destroyed, just unidentifiable.

One thing I was worried about was their baby boxes. I had kept everything in those—their photos, the outfits they wore home from the hospital, their baby books, even report cards and sports awards. I was frantic because I wanted those baby boxes. I could find only Kilee's. The top was burned, but everything was in it.

I stood there crying, trying to piece everything together. *How did she make it out of here? Why couldn't it have been me? Why couldn't I have been there? Why didn't she text me and ask me if she should light a candle?*

But you can't dwell on it. It happened, and you have to move on. But you just want to make sense of it.

Cameron and I were in there for a while. We were just trying to see what we could find. There were a lot of sentimental things we were looking for—little things. His room was destroyed. I was heartbroken.

The fire was ruled an accident by the fire chief Monday night, but we were still interrogated for two hours by the adjuster. It's the procedure they have to follow—even though they knew it wasn't arson, it's policy, and that was the way it had to be done. He even teared up when talking to us about what happened. I couldn't imagine having his job, dealing with people every day who have lost so much.

There seemed to be hundreds of questions that he had to ask. Wade got angry at all the questioning. I just touched his leg and reassured him that the insurance company was there to help us.

We were eager to get back to the hospital. Kilee's first surgery was the next day. And after spending a day seeing everything we had lost, we wanted to get back to sit with the person we didn't lose and were so grateful for.

Thirty-Eight Days at Shriners

Every day, Kilee said, "I want to go home."

As a mother, when you get to Shriners, you kind of prepare yourself—if that's even possible.

In the back of your mind you think, *OK, there could be some scares throughout this, but let's keep our fingers crossed and hope and pray that nothing happens. Hopefully she can just completely heal each day and not have any complications.*

The rare times when she would say, "I can't do this," I would tell her, "Kilee, there's a reason why you're here. This is something we may never understand or even ever explain, but you're here, and that is all that matters. You are alive; none of the rest matters. You are alive and you're here."

I got to the point where I was numb to all the pain she was dealing with. I couldn't let it get to me anymore because as soon as I walked into the room, I knew she was in pain. It was hard for me to handle mentally. That's my child. You never want to see your child go through that.

The number-one goal was to get her better and get her out of there. Forget about the scars and get her better and move on. *This is our life now,* I thought, *so let's deal with it.*

Lazy Eye

When Kilee was two, her doctor noticed that her right eye was lazy at a checkup.

An optometrist diagnosed her as having a lazy eye. She was prescribed glasses to try to correct it. We tried a patch over the eye for years. As therapy, Kilee would string Cheerios with a needle and thread with the good eye closed. We did it for years, but nothing corrected it; her vision remained blurry.

We accepted it. It never held Kilee back in sports or school or anything. Years later, she started wearing a contact lens in that eye. Her other eye is 20/20.

It's her contact lens that saved her lazy eye in the explosion. They removed the piece of plastic from her "good eye" and treated her eye with antibiotic drips. After two weeks of cream and medicine in Shriners, her eye was healed and as good as new.

Kilee's Spirit Check

Before Kilee went into any surgeries, a psychologist came in to prepare us, the parents. Of course, he had seen Kilee only the way she looked in the hospital. She was swollen and she appeared fifty pounds heavier. She was bandaged up, and her face was pretty burned. Her feet were uncovered, and they were badly burned. There were burn holes on the top of both of her feet. I'm sure he's used to that and deals with patients like Kilee all the time—he's worked there for decades.

He talked to Kilee to assess her and see how her spirits were. It is beyond me how they can consider what a kid's attitude should be when she is lying in a hospital bed, burned, bandaged, and heavily medicated.

The psychologist told us he was going to go over some steps for us, as parents, to help Kilee. He told us about different phases of what Kilee would be able to do and how she would cope. He warned us that she was likely to struggle and be depressed. Listening to all he was saying, the reality of Kilee's future was beginning to set in. Yet we still didn't know how bad it was or would be. We tried to comprehend everything the doctor said, but it felt like a setback before we'd even started her recovery.

We wanted to get Kilee into surgery and see how she'd do. We didn't know if she would be able to use her hands, arms, or legs. No one went into depth about what she would or would not have, or could or could not do.

The psychologist had a very dry personality. There was no laughing or joking. He was very to the point. He told us to prepare, get ourselves in order, and be strong for Kilee. When he said that to Jason and me, he had assumed we were married. Once we corrected him, he asked a ton of questions about living arrangements—where we were going to live, who would care for Kilee, and so on.

He got to me at the very end and he looked at me and said, nonchalantly, "So, how are you doing?"

I looked at Jason. I looked back at the doctor. I was thinking, *Why is he singling me out?* "I'm doing as well as I can, I guess."

"Been eating?"

"No, not really. I haven't really had an appetite."

"You've been sleeping?"

"Maybe a couple of hours a night—doing the best I can right now."

"You have to get yourself in order, or she'll never heal right."

"Do I look that bad?" I asked.

He just lowered his head and looked over his glasses at me.

It made me realize I needed to sleep, eat, and take a shower. It was an eye-opener, a clear sign that I needed to pull myself together. I looked like I had lost about ten pounds in those three days at Shriners, and the people who knew me were worried.

It was the wake-up call I needed. I had to be strong mentally, emotionally, and physically for Kilee.

❧

Kilee:

The psychologist was an older man. He would always come in and sit down and talk. I didn't want to talk to him at all.

"I'm fine, guys. I don't need to talk to him," I'd tell my parents.

He was there to figure out what medications I needed to take for depression. He would come in and ask me all kinds of questions. "How are you feeling today? How have you felt in the past four days? Are you feeling sad or happy?"

Every time he came to see me, he told me it was normal to feel sad and scared, and that I could talk to him about it and he wouldn't tell anyone what I said.

I told him, "I'm fine. I'm fine." I wasn't really scared, I just didn't want to talk about it with him.

The situation seemed odd to me. I had never met this man before. To me, he was just some random guy. How was I supposed to talk to him about my deepest feelings?

Everything Is Temporary

Lori:

Kilee was in the ICU for seven days. She didn't want to be alone, so Jason and I took shifts to be with her. We at least got a few hours of sleep every night that way. But whoever was in the room with her did not sleep. After her catheter was taken out, Kilee was always up. She had to pee constantly. It was difficult even to get her out of bed. And there were times she didn't make it to the toilet, because it was hard for her to walk. She was wobbly and weak and her feet were damaged.

Initially, her night-shift nurse came across as very bold, maybe a bit overwhelming. But we learned to really, really like her. She was Kilee's strength. She would tell Kilee what they were going to do and why. She was stern and straight with her. There was no sugarcoating anything, but she definitely had compassion. You could tell she really cared.

She was in her mid-thirties and always had a different hair color. Once it was pink. It was really cute, and it was her hair that broke the ice with us. I told her how much I loved her hair. Kilee had always wanted to dye her ends pink, and I wouldn't let her. And now her nurse had pink hair.

She would tell Kilee, "This is temporary. This is all temporary."

Those words have stuck with us. They became the mantra that got us through so many hard days and dark nights. Things were painful, but they were temporary. Things were difficult, but they were temporary. Even when it seemed that our whole world was stuck in the ashes of that fire, these words strengthened us: This is temporary.

Her scars are forever, but Kilee's physical struggles were temporary.

The Surgeries

Kilee:

I don't remember a lot from Shriners. It's probably best that way.

The day of one of my surgeries, they rolled my bed down the hallway to the operating room. Many people surrounded me as I was wheeled toward the operating room. The doctors pushed me through the doors…and everyone else stayed on the other side. They couldn't go beyond the doors.

It was hot in the room; at least 100 degrees. I don't know how they did surgery it was so hot. They laid me on a table and put a mask on my face. They told me it was OK to close my eyes and that I wouldn't remember anything.

However, I do remember that after the surgery, they wrapped my whole body in this stuff, like a mushy Velcro suit. It was gross. It didn't hurt, but it gave me the most disgusting feeling ever. They came in every day, every single hour and poured water inside of it to keep everything wet— letting the water just sit. It felt nasty. It just sat inside of it.

Before the surgery, I wasn't in any pain. I didn't feel much of anything. It just felt normal. I knew I wasn't fine because I was going into surgery, but I felt OK. I never thought, *Oh, this is really, really bad.*

I just figured since I was in the hospital, I was there for a reason; something must be wrong. I didn't know how bad it was.

My life was about to get really hard.

Lori:

We stayed the entire thirty-eight days with Kilee in Shriners. The hardest parts were the surgeries and the scares that we had. Three days into her stay, Dr. Kagan said to expect one day in Shriners for each percentage she was burned, which would mean we would be there for forty-five days.

Prepping her for surgery, they put her in a surgical cap and gown and sedated her in her room. When they were about to wheel her to surgery, we told Kilee we loved her, and even though her eyes were open, they were glazed over because of her medication. It was definitely one of the hardest things to witness, to see my child go through that.

They prepared us by telling us the chances and the risks involved in the surgery. They told us they would do the best they could do with her—but with every surgery there is life-threatening risk. There could be complications. Basically, they told us, *This is what could happen, but we are keeping our fingers crossed that it won't.* Of course, they said it much more medically than that.

The first surgery took two or three hours. They were stripping all of Kilee's skin and damaged tissue from the areas that would be grafted—her hands, arms, and abdomen—cleaning it up and putting a tube of water hooked up to a cloth in those areas to keep the skin wet. Every hour after surgery, the doctors had to pump the inside of her bandages full of liquid so the skin graft would take. They also had to keep bacteria out and prevent infection. Kilee could feel it, and it was repulsive to her. She was wet and cold all the time.

The staff told us the first surgery was successful. They'd gotten her cleaned up and her breathing was fine. They were ready for the next surgery the following day, to do the first set of skin grafts, taking skin from Kilee's upper back and thighs and grafting it onto the most damaged areas of her body. Kilee was heavily sedated through her next surgery; I think they did that so she wouldn't have to remember that pain. It must have been excruciating.

The next surgery, on Friday, November 14, followed the same process. The doctors talked to us about what was going to happen, and we waited for three hours.

I cried most of that time. We knew this was the procedure that was going to make or break whether Kilee would have use of her hands and keep her fingertips. We didn't know how much they would get done in the surgery and if they'd need more donor sites because of how severe the burns were. It was difficult sitting there thinking about all the what-ifs.

What if she can't throw a ball? What if she can't play soccer again? Just as the worst worries would consume us, we would stop and think, *It's OK. She's alive. She's here.*

Things turned out better than we'd thought they might. Kilee's fingertips were saved in surgery. They did not have to graft the palms of her hands, as they'd thought they would. Both of her arms, entirely up to her shoulders, were grafted, as well as her stomach, where she had one of her worst burns.

Once the skin on her thighs and back were replenished, Dr. Kagan told us he would move on to phase two of Kilee's surgeries.

"Essentially, you're trying to make cakes for fourteen people, but the oven only holds two cakes. So you have to stage things," was what Dr. Kagan told us about skin grafting.

There were still a lot of places that needed work done, and it was unsure whether the doctors were going to be able to fix them with skin grafts. The skin on Kilee's bottom, both calves, her lower back, and her ankles was deteriorating.

The next five days were horrible. Kilee could not get out of bed. She was on her back the entire time.

On the fourth day after surgery, Kilee got an infection in her back at the donor site. She had gauze on with medication underneath it, then wrapped up with an Ace bandage. When the nurses checked, it was green and milky. It was bad.

In that situation, the donor site could actually require another surgery. It's very dangerous and can cause a lot of complications. Not only that, but the doctors needed that skin to be healthy so it could be used again for more grafts on other parts of Kilee's body. If it didn't heal right, they wouldn't be able to use it. We were told that if her back didn't heal, doctors could take skin from Kilee's scalp. That freaked me out.

Will she have hair? She'd already been shaved because her hair was singed. It was scary. She's a girl, and she wanted her long hair back. It was going to be a long road already, and while that should have been the furthest thing from our minds, it made us think about Kilee losing another piece of herself. At one point, I even said, "Give her my skin."

Any time they cleaned her infected donor site and bathed her, Kilee screamed the entire time. It took four hours. There was green on her back, on her leg. Her ankles and her feet were swollen from infection and fluids. Her size-eight feet ballooned to a size eleven or twelve. She's a 110-pound girl who looked to be 150 pounds.

This was the first time we had seen her unwrapped at all. Before, all we could see was her fingers, which were burnt to a crisp and black. We could see her face and part of her neck. When they got to her buttocks, it was the worst of her burns. She screamed and screamed and screamed the whole time we were in there. Just screamed. It was awful knowing she had to go through that. It took a few days and a lot of pain and blood-curdling screams, but they cleaned up her back for the next surgery.

Every day, twice a day, Kilee had to have a bath, and the screaming continued. It was just dreadful. I'll never forget that sound as long as I live—her screams, the nurses trying to calm her down. I'll never forget that.

The fifth day after surgery, we saw Kilee's arms.

To prepare us for what her skin might look like in the future, they showed us a book. There were a lot of examples of what to expect after skin grafts, three months, six months, nine months, and twelve months later. Most of the people in the book who had skin grafts had blackened-looking arms. It was pretty scary. But when we saw her arms for the first time, there were seams—tons of seams—like skin patchwork with staples all over her to keep it in place. And it was tan. She had just been to the beach, and since they used her back as a donor site, it was a different shade than her arms. They looked good, though, compared to those in the book. Her skin graft took to her arms 100 percent, and that doesn't happen that often.

Community Relations

Shriners asked us if we wanted to do an interview with the media. We couldn't even fathom it. We were worried about Kilee still and how she was doing, and we didn't want to allow anyone to invade her privacy. So they asked us what to say so they could give a statement to the media. They took care of it for us.

And while Wade and I were taking care of our totaled house and insurance investigators, Jason was updating the public about Kilee's condition in Shriners on CaringBridge. People were reaching out on social media with #PrayersForKilee, so we thought they should know how she was doing.

November 12, 2014
9:12 PM

Kilee is a patient at Shriners Hospitals for Children in Cincinnati. She has second- and third-degree burns on 45 percent of her body. Surgery is planned for Thursday and Friday of this week. She is doing well for her first few days in the hospital. While Kilee sleeps a lot, when she is awake, she enjoys talking to us. Most of all, Kilee enjoys her mixed fruit juice the best.

November 14, 2014
4:26 AM

As I sit here watching Kilee sleep, I can't help but wonder what she's thinking. I've never been in a position where I am unable to help my child. We sit here watching over her every day, she knows we love her, and we tell her about all the community support she is receiving. Through all the medication, she still manages a slight smile to let you know she's listening. Though I can see the pain in her eyes, they still sparkle. This morning is a big step toward recovery. First skin graft. I would be lying to say I'm not scared. But Kilee isn't. I've never met a braver, stronger person. I am proud to be able to say she's my daughter.

November 17, 2014
4:37 PM

Kilee is doing much better. She received good news today from the optometrist and the respiratory therapist. Her eye is almost healed and they removed the corrective contact. Respiratory said she is breathing much better and changed her oxygen mask to one she likes better. Kilee says, "Thank you" to everybody who's been concerned about her. "It means a lot."

November 18, 2014
12:51 PM

Late entry today…I wasn't able to get a break, as this morning after 6:00 AM Kilee started feeling bad and uncomfortable. As good as she was yesterday, this morning was the opposite. Health-wise, she is doing OK. Her breathing is improving; all vitals seem relatively stable. It was pain from her surgically repaired areas and her stomach was hurting. This morning's bath was hard on her too. Cleaning her wounds is like pouring salt onto them. She is now resting in bed and receiving some medication to ease her pain. For now, we are good.

November 20, 2014
7:03 AM

Good news! On Wednesday the doctor examined Kilee's grafts and said they look good, two thumbs up! Each day, twice a day, they clean all her sites. Excruciating pain from her donor sites. Her arms are sore and sensitive as they heal. Today Kilee is going to try a wheelchair to take a ride around the hospital. A change of scenery to get out of her room for a while.

Bathing

Lori:

Eventually, the nurses told us we would have to give Kilee her baths soon.

What? I thought. *Wait, no, that's your job.*

But we soon learned that it was our preparation for when she went home. We had to bathe her, wrap her, and act as her nurses at home. And that was why they insisted on us being in the room while she was getting bathed and wrapped after her surgeries. In the beginning, they want the parents out of the room to grieve. It also helps the child to be stronger if the parents are not in there; it keeps the child from latching on to the parents instead of finding his or her own strength to get through everything. But once Kilee was a little further along, past her surgeries, we needed to be involved in the next chapter in her recovery process.

It was a time when we, too, were a little stronger and could be sterner with Kilee. We told her she had to do whatever the nurses told her to do. On days when she would say she couldn't, we had to tell her, "Yes, you can and you have to. If you want to get through this, you have to do it."

Once we stopped feeling bad for her and stopped sugarcoating everything, Kilee got stronger. It wasn't easy to be that stern with her. As soon as I would leave the room, I would find a place to cry.

Praying Away the Pain

The physical therapist came in for the first time, and Kilee could not move her hands at all. It was unbelievable. She couldn't do a lot that day, but they talked about the plan and what she would do going forward.

She had therapy three times a day, but it depended on how long her baths took. One day, her bath took six hours—six straight hours with all of the same nurses and assistants. It was horrendous. She was in great pain. She screamed many times.

Using tweezers, they were picking the scabs from her arms, a little at a time. That part didn't hurt her; in fact, she was mesmerized by it. Her arms felt good. Dr. Kagan had told us she would feel good where she had been grafted.

So we wanted to get that part done so she felt better all over. Her bottom, her back, and her legs were still very painful for her. She was having horrible pain in her calf, and they were still trying to heal the oozing, green infection on her back.

I've always said a prayer with Kilee and Cameron every night before they go to sleep. They were raised in church from the time they were little, but Kilee has never been an outwardly religious person. But that day, she was in such excruciating pain that out of the blue she stopped everything and said, "I want to say a prayer."

She started to pray about four hours into the bath.

It was a long prayer, and I cannot even begin to tell you what she said, but basically, she was pleading, "Please God, get me through this." She broke down crying.

Everyone in the room was crying as she went on.

"I know I can do this. I know I'm a strong person," Kilee said.

Everyone said, "Amen," when she finished.

An Unexpected Scare

The nurses and Dr. Kagan thought Kilee might have a blood clot in her calf, which would have explained the extreme pain she was feeling in her leg during her bath. They rushed her over to Children's to get it checked out. It was the worst pain she'd felt. It was bad. She cried most of the day. She cried and cried and cried. No screaming, just constant crying because it was just hurting her so badly.

I was nervous.

We got to Children's and they told us they needed to do an ultrasound on her leg. As they were doing the ultrasound, Kilee screamed so loudly that I heard her from the waiting room. They came out and told us they were going to have to try something else because she couldn't handle the pain. The nurses were crying—it was that horrific. The doctor told us there was a slim chance of it working, but they could do a CT scan. There was also a small chance, he told us, that if it was a blood clot, it could kill her.

Our worst fears came back into play like the first night of the explosion. I kept thinking that after everything that had gone on, this just couldn't happen. Your mind just goes there. *We just want her here; we just want her here.*

We were out of options because of Kilee's extreme pain. Every little bump and movement was agonizing for her.

Blood clots are common in skin grafts and burns. A clot could have killed her or at least complicated the healing process for her.

Dr. Kagan approved the procedure from Shriners. It took forty-five minutes to get Kilee prepped while we sat in yet another waiting room and quietly sobbed.

When they were ready for her, we stood beside her, Jason on one side, me on the other. Wade was in the room as well. We held her hands and waited for it to be over as they sent her through the machine.

It took nearly the rest of the day to get her results. There were no blood clots. They never could tell us what it was that had caused Kilee so much pain. It could have been an infection trying to brew inside because her leg was three times its normal size, but they just couldn't find anything.

On December 4, Kilee underwent a similar skin-cleaning procedure and the next day received her second skin graft on her buttocks, calf, ankles, and lower back.

Closer as a Family

I felt helpless watching Kilee in pain.

She hardly smiled the entire time, other than the last few days leading to her release. She was in so much pain and discomfort; she was unable to see the miraculous changes she was undergoing. Smiles for me came often when I saw her progress in healing or watched her determination to make it through physical therapy and the dreaded bath times. I smiled every time I saw her move past a goal such as walking, sitting up, and using her hands and arms.

She's the one who was healing and will continue to heal her entire life—but we were all healing with her. You just get tighter as a family. We were close before, but this definitely changed us—for the better.

Wade loves my kids. He's just one of those people who doesn't express feelings by outward displays. He's not all about hugging and stuff like that. Instead, he and Kilee fist bump. When Kilee was in the hospital, everyone was different, closer. The little things that maybe you wouldn't normally do, you do.

I think it's part of accepting what is going on and what will happen, as a family, and going from there. It's like Kilee calling us "Mommy" and "Daddy" in the hospital. Or her saying "I love you" to Houstin and Collin and Wade. Very few people saw her in her room, but she allowed them inside. That was a big thing for her to even allow them into her room and let them into her recovery. It was a vulnerable time for her physically and emotionally.

You definitely do get tighter as a family. I always thought we were close before. We would always get together as often as we could as a whole family. I just hoped the newfound closeness wouldn't go away. I wanted to keep it like that and keep that special bond Wade will always have with my kids.

Hidden Scars: A Change in Me

Kilee had a nurse that had short hair, and that nurse told her she loved Kilee's short hair. Kilee told her she liked the nurse's hair as well, but that her own short hair wasn't by choice. This was the first time Kilee expressed her feelings about not having hair.

Her hair had been beautiful, but it was gone. Still, her beauty exuded through her smile, her attitude, and her perseverance. Hair didn't define her beauty—inside or out.

On day ten, Kilee took her next push forward, seeing something she had not seen in nearly two weeks: her own reflection. She was leery of seeing what her face looked like. She took a minute checking herself out: red spots on her face, shaved head, and no eyelashes. She looked over at her nurse and me, shrugged her shoulders, and simply said, "OK."

Kilee:

Shriners changed me.

I may not remember most of my stay at Shriners, but everything I was scared of there is very memorable to me. I remember how it felt to know that nothing was going to be the same. It was confusing and hard. Imagine being sixteen years old, finally getting more freedom than you've ever had in your life, and then having it all taken away from you. Your hands, arms, body, hair, face, and in some cases, your self-esteem. You are in the hospital, not at school with your friends or even at home. And on top of everything, when you are finally coming off medications, you realize you don't have your own home, any of your own clothes, or any of the things that make you comfortable.

I never thought I would have to go through any of those things; I never even knew those things existed. I never thought about any of that stuff. I never thought I would look any different throughout my whole life. I grew to love my body, and I was very content with the way I looked. I was really beginning to love my hair—that was one of the main things people complimented when they saw me.

I was grateful and thankful that I was alive, but I was set on always looking that way. In a way, I was disappointed and upset that I would never look at myself and see the same thing I'd finally learned to love. I didn't even have my hair, which was hard to accept.

Everything changed.

I looked different. I couldn't wear anything I wanted for the longest time. Like most teenagers, I loved expressing myself through my clothes, but I couldn't do that in Shriners. I had to wear pressure garments that covered every inch of my body, except my toes and head. They were very uncomfortable. They weren't attractive in any way.

My body wasn't the same. I couldn't move the same way or do the things I had always done. I had burns, turning into scars, everywhere. I couldn't feel the same. I looked in the mirror and wondered, *Why me?* I didn't see any of the person I used to look like in the mirror. I couldn't understand. I went from being content with myself to confused and uncertain about who I was and who I was going to be.

Now that a little time has passed, I think of everything as not that big of a deal. I know that I won't ever look as good as I did before, but I can get pretty close, and that is fine with me. I am just grateful to be alive and well. And I know who to thank for that: Digger.

CHAPTER FOUR

A Girl's Best Friend

Kilee:

When I think back to the explosion, I think about Digger.

I was ten when we got Digger and Doogie. They're Chihuahua-Yorkshire terriers, or "Chorkies." They were these little puppies, one white and one black, wrapped in a blanket in a basket, and they were incredibly tiny.

Digger and Doogie were born to a family friend's dog, and we were asked if we wanted a puppy. The pups were adorable and they fit in my hand.

Even though they are brothers from the same litter, they couldn't be more different. Digger is really smart, knows everything that is going on around him, is very loving, and thinks of himself as a watchdog. Even as a puppy, Digger was very aware of his surroundings. He can do any trick you tell him to (except get the newspaper).

Doogie is not nearly as smart as Digger, and he is a bit lazier. Lying around all day is his favorite pastime. Ever since we got them, Digger has been the playful one, running around, chewing on bones and toys, and having fun. Doogie...not so much. He likes to lie on the couch and sleep mostly.

We were going to get just one. Wade agreed to just one.

೪೦೪

Lori:

Wade and I were just moving in together and thought it was a good time to get a family dog.

That day, I was picking up Doogie from a friend whose dog had just had puppies. There were only two dogs in the litter. The dad was a white Chihuahua, and the mom was a purebred Yorkshire terrier. We had to decide which puppy to take. I loved Doogie, and there was no way we could handle two dogs. But my friend was having a hard time finding a home for Digger. I had said something previously to Wade about getting both dogs, and he didn't seem too fond of the idea.

I strategically planned the next step: How was I going to get both dogs?

I came home and put them both into a laundry basket. They were six weeks old and teeny. Wade came home from work, and I told him I had something for him. I hadn't told him it was the day I was supposed to pick up Doogie. I put the laundry basket up on the bed to reveal his surprise.

He said, "Oh my gosh, did you get both of them? Are you serious?"

"Come on, he's so cute and we love him…"

That's all it took. Wade was hooked. It was love at first sight.

Doogie is a small eight pounds, is bashful and shy, and just wants to lie on your lap.

Digger, named for his love of digging in the dirt, is 14.5 pounds of muscle, is active, and likes to play and chew bones. And he's super smart. He can pretty much do any trick you teach him. He's one of those dogs that will bark when anyone comes to the house. He's always been protective of the house—not necessarily of each of us, but the house. Before the accident, the opportunity for Digger to protect one of us had never really come up.

He's pretty close to Kilee. He's always with her, in her room, wanting to know where she is and what she's doing. When she gets home, he always runs to her.

We never realized how incredibly smart Digger truly was.

My Savior

Kilee:

When I got home on the day of the explosion, I let the dogs out of the bathroom, where they had been all day. That's when I smelled that horrible odor. I let the dogs outside, and about five minutes later, I let them back inside and they sat on the couch with me.

Digger always sits up on top of the couch to look out the window, keeping a watchful eye on the neighborhood, traffic, and the occasional squirrel.

When I got up, both Digger and Doogie stayed on the couch. While I made my way to the kitchen drawer and then to the bathroom, they stayed put. Doogie napped on the couch while Digger was still on the lookout.

A flash and a boom!

I was knocked out cold.

Then Digger started barking, going crazy. Once he woke me up, I got up and started staggering and trying to run out the back door to the deck. Digger was by my side the entire time, barking, almost like an SOS. He barked at me, following me around to the neighbors' and to the pavement where I finally sat. It's like he knew there was something going on and something seriously wrong with me. He had a sense that it was not right. He would not calm down at all. He ran around me as people arrived and continued barking, alerting people that there was something wrong with me.

He never left my side. He sat with me the whole time waiting on my mom and the ambulance.

Ever since the accident, he is always with me at home. He watches out for me now, and if anyone were to hurt me, he would go crazy. He knows what happened, and he tries to protect me in any way he can.

Lori:

After the explosion, Doogie hid, but Digger stayed with Kilee. He literally risked his life to stay with her and bark until she came to and then ran out of the house by her side. He saved her life.

When I reached Kilee, Digger was protecting her. Even against me and others who were trying to help Kilee. I yelled at him, "Digger, you've got to stop!"

He just circled Kilee the entire time we were outside with her—just circling her and circling her and circling her, and barking at her. He wouldn't leave her alone, nor would he listen to us. He just couldn't get himself together.

We know Kilee wouldn't be here today with us if not for Digger.

Thank God for that dog.

Wade's sons, Collin and Houstin, brought Digger to Shriners to see us the day after we got there. Seeing him was like seeing a miracle. He saved my family.

You take things and life for granted every day, and you don't even realize you're doing it.

Kilee talked about Digger a lot while she was in Shriners. She knew that him being there that day was the reason she survived. The explosion blew the windows and doors out of the house. He could've run away, but he didn't. He stayed. And he ultimately saved her life.

While Kilee was in the hospital, Digger was a mess. He was always running around in circles, looking for Kilee, waiting for her.

Once we brought Kilee home, Digger went nuts. She was packed in all her pressure garments and had no hair.

He sniffed her forever. It was the first time she had seen him since the fire, and she sat with him and consoled him, telling him, "Oh, it's OK, buddy. It's OK."

He seemed confused because she looked so different, but he knew it was her and he kept smelling her. He just kept sniffing her fingers and her head—probably for the next two months.

One time, he couldn't get into her room with her, and he was digging hard on her door. I was helping Kilee get her garments on after her bath and my hand slipped and I accidentally scratched her. She screamed and cried so loudly that Digger freaked out.

He's always anxious now. He can't sit still. If Kilee's sitting there, he's right next to her. He would get protective of her if she yelled during and after her baths. He had to be in there to make sure she was OK. He slept with her often and still does today.

Kilee:

When I came home, Digger sniffed me forever, like an hour, trying to figure out where I had been. And from that moment, he's been by my side. After my showers when I have to put lotion on, he sits on the floor next to my bed and watches the entire time. It's as though he's asking me, "What are you doing?" and "Why are you doing it?" He can't understand, but he's doing what he can to make sure I'm OK.

He changed from the family pet to my lifesaver, my dog. He's my protector.

If not for Digger jumping into action, I probably would not have gotten up after the explosion, and I probably would not have gotten out of the house that day. I'm here today because of Digger.

CHAPTER FIVE

Struggling to Be Me

Kilee:

When I turned sixteen, I got my driver's license. I got a car. I gained the freedom I had been dreaming of my entire teen life. Now, I couldn't even go to the bathroom on my own. My independence was gone in an instant, and it wasn't an easy pill to swallow.

Baby Steps to Independence

Lori:

Therapy started after day five of her graft. Kilee had very limited mobility, barely able to move her hands, her arms—in all honesty, she couldn't even move her legs. She couldn't walk. They waited a couple of days before they got her up and walked her outside of her room.

When they finally got her up to walk, there was a place outside of her room within walking distance—twenty steps, which seemed like 500 steps for her. It took Kilee ten minutes to walk those twenty steps.

They were setting goals for her. They started small, just walking down the hall, making it to the wall. Eventually those twenty steps felt less like 500 steps and more like 150. There was a significant gain in how mobile Kilee was.

She had therapy three times a day. The third time for the day was at night, and Jason and I had to start doing that around day ten.

It was hard because we did not know what the outcome was going to be.

Shriners employees deal with this every day. They see the progress and they know what the long-term results will be. They watch a lot of children leave their care and lead normal lives.

They also work with children who struggle much more and take longer to heal. They try to prepare you, to tell you what to expect. But nothing can really prepare you.

It's incredible that that is what they have to do and see every day. I couldn't imagine dealing with that every day of my life. It takes a really special person to do that job, and I am grateful that we found special people with the strength and skill to help us in our worst crisis.

Kilee didn't have just one special person. She had twenty-five special people at Shriners throughout the process. They are there to help, and they know what to do.

I didn't. I just kept thinking, *Is she going to be OK? What limitations will she have? What can she do now? What can she do later?*

Her hands were the biggest piece to her healing process. When they graft you like that, and you literally have nothing but tissue showing to start and no muscle at all, you have to relearn how to do everything.

There wasn't a day that Kilee didn't scream at least twice, sometimes more, from the pain that came with therapy, bathing, and sitting in a wheelchair. After her bottom was grafted, it was so tender, so painful, that she couldn't do anything.

After that graft, they had her lie on her belly for a while. All the extra fluids in her body rushed to her face. Every day, her face would get bigger and bigger. She was so swollen that it looked as though she had gained about fifty pounds.

Every day, Kilee would scream. Every day, she would hear other kids in that unit screaming. It was a lot of the little kids. I would just sit there and think about all the pain she was going through, and I thought there was no way she would forget that pain. There's no way.

As an adult, when you break your leg, your arm, whatever, you don't forget that pain. You know how bad that hurts. Having a baby—you know what that feels like. You don't forget that pain.

I just don't want her to remember how much it all hurt. Emotionally, how is she going to be OK from all of this? How is she going to be able to cope knowing all of the pain she went through?

The lucky thing is, she did forget. She remembers only bits and pieces of her time at Shriners.

Weaning from the Pain

After her first surgery, but before her second, the doctors started to wean Kilee off her medications. She was up and alert for a couple of hours every night.

They kept her comfortable, but it's not healthy for kids to be heavily medicated for a long period of time, especially with pain medication. She was also on anxiety medication for pain and depression. To me, it seemed unnecessary because Kilee started to get emotional at least once a day, which just wasn't like her. She would look at me with a tear in her eye and say she didn't even know why she was upset. It was the drugs talking. So I was glad to see her coming off some of those medications. I was starting to get a glimpse of the old Kilee again.

I just wanted to make sure that, with all of the drugs, this wasn't the beginning of the end with Kilee. I had worked for years with people in recovery, and I knew how easy it was for an experience like this to have permanent consequences. I couldn't live with myself if her mental health were jeopardized. I finally expressed my concerns to the psychologist before Kilee's second set of surgeries.

I explained that Kilee seemed flat. Her personality was dulled. She never laughed or even giggled. She never showed much emotion. She looked angry all the time. "Smiley Kilee" never smiled. It was night and day from her normal personality. And I knew the reason was the medication. I had zero doubts about that.

That's when her doctor started weaning her off the meds. Once Kilee was off the medication, it was a remarkable transformation.

"Crippled" with Fear

Kilee:

The biggest obstacles I've overcome are getting better and being able to tell myself that I can do these things. I am proud of myself and happy with everything I have overcome. I never would have imagined I could do any of this; and I have proved myself, and everyone around me, wrong.

After my first surgery, I was lying in my bed on my stomach, and before I got my pressure garments, my therapists would wrap Coban, a sort of stretchy adhesive bandage, around my hand. But first, they would try to stretch out my hand and fingers. Stretching my skin felt like if you pull on your skin as far as it will go—and that was if I just touched it. It was painful, and I would say, "That's enough." They would tell me I had to do it anyway—no matter how much it hurt. They did it every day, three or four times a day. It was exhausting, and I was miserable. It felt like someone was always in my room, telling me it was "time to stretch." They said it was the only way for me to get better. They had to stretch my hands, even when—especially when—I didn't want to.

Every morning, I had a routine. I had to wake up at 7:30. Without fail, my occupational therapist would come in at eight, take off my sleeves, rub lotion up and down my arms, and stretch my hands. I had that done three times a day, sometimes for two hours each time.

But one day, my regular therapist was off.

The therapist filling in was running all over the room, washing her hands really fast, coming over to me and telling me she'd be there in a minute and not to worry. This is not what I was used to with my regular therapist. My usual therapist worked at my pace and helped me when I needed it.

Normally, I would sit in the chair and my therapist would sit in a chair right beside me. There'd be a table in front of me where I would rest my arms and hands. Then, she would put lotion on me and start stretching.

The new therapist was different. She put the lotion on me and stretched me. Then she stood up in front of me and looked down at me and told me I needed to raise my arm. I had already told her I couldn't do that. My back was hurting and my regular therapist was fine with me not doing it yet. But this new therapist started in on me, telling me I had to do it. She just kept going and going, and I told her I couldn't. Even my mom and dad chimed in and told her I couldn't do it yet and my regular therapist was OK with that.

I couldn't raise my arms because they had just taken skin from my back and there was still this cotton stuff on it. If I moved the wrong way, it pinched me. If I raised my arms, it pinched the whole side of my back. I told the therapist I wasn't going to raise my arms this time. I didn't have any burns under my arms, so really, there was no reason for me to stretch that part of my arms. Or, so I thought. The therapist told me my skin could start banding and that's why it was so important to do those stretches.

The therapist told me that if I didn't progress, there was a possibility I could be crippled.

I was already upset because I didn't want to do it and she was trying to force me. I did one side, but then I could not do the other. I was crying. I was angry.

We quit for the day.

Lori:

I knew her arms would get better and better. But at that point, she couldn't even lift her arms up. But I figured it had to come back up at some point. I'm somewhat of an overachiever, so I had instilled that in her as well, and I kept telling her she had to do this.

"You have to lift your arm, Kilee."

She was exhausted from nonstop therapy, going to the teen room, baths twice a day—just one thing right after another. "So much to do, so little time" never rang truer. Kilee would tell me, "I just want to sit here. I don't want to move my hands. I don't want to get up. I don't want to walk, and I really don't want to hang out in the teen room."

But "not doing" wasn't an option.

We knew her personality before this, but the Shriners team didn't. So when she would say she was tired and didn't want to do something, they would come back at her, saying, "It doesn't matter what you want to do. You have to do it to get better."

That was hard for me. I knew Kilee was doing the best she could; she was overwhelmed. I wanted to say, "Just let her chill out for a minute, let her regroup, and then we'll come back."

Whenever we tried to object, we'd hear, "Well, we have a schedule, and we need to do this, this, and this. We don't have time to come back."

The next day, that same therapist came into Kilee's room at 9:30 in the morning.

Kilee had her arm sitting on the chair, and she made a noise when the therapist started pushing on her. Something like, "uhhh."

The therapist turned to Kilee and said, "'Uhhh'? I don't know what 'uhhh' is! You have to talk to me about this! You have to tell me what's going on! I have no idea what's going on! If you don't start doing this and progressing, you could be crippled!"

I looked at her and I said, "You've got to give her a minute. You're not going to get anywhere with Kilee that way. Kilee's personality is not like that. She is not confrontational. Please just give her a moment."

Jason and I just about lost it at that point. Of course, I was crying. He had tears in his eyes. Kilee was crying out of frustration.

As she was saying this stuff to us, I was worried that maybe Kilee's progress wasn't as good as others had been telling us. Could she really be crippled and not able to use her hands and arms? I had a lot of emotions rushing through my mind, and I was trying to be strong for Kilee.

So I stopped. I looked at Kilee, and I said to her, "No. You take a few minutes and you do this for you because you want to heal. You don't do this for anyone else. You do this for you."

When I said that, she completely changed her demeanor, and she slowly started her exercises with the therapist.

It was like a wake-up call for Kilee. Someone talking to her like that motivated her to fight even harder than she already had been. We told her, "You do it on your time, your pace. But know that you need to do it."

I think she realized that this is what had to happen for her to go home. And that's when "I want to go home" really started from Kilee.

In hindsight, it was essential that Kilee did what the therapist told her to do. Maybe Kilee didn't handle it the right way. But we had to have the realization that there was only one way for Kilee to recover in the long run: Do what they tell you to do.

ৎ৵ ৵ৎ

Kilee:

When they took out my feeding tube, they were freaking out. It was at night. It wasn't my regular nurse, and I didn't want to do it without her. We had been close. She did everything. But this nurse crushed up my pills and was putting them down my feeding tube when they got stuck.

She was getting mad at the pills. She squeezed the tube, but they wouldn't budge. Then she talked to the other nurses. She wanted to take out my feeding tube, but I still needed it to get all of the calories because I couldn't eat.

They told me they were going to have to take it out. I didn't want them to. It was all the way down my throat. But they took it out through my nose. I could feel it coming up my throat. It choked me and I couldn't breathe for a minute. It was awful.

From then on, I ate food.

Eventually, I could visit the suites where my parents stayed at Shriners and eat with them. They tried to get me to eat everything, but nothing tasted good at all.

Relearning Normal

Walking for the first time was really hard. I felt like an old grandma trying to get up out of bed. It didn't hurt, but one of my legs couldn't bend, so I was dragging my foot. I was trying to walk to the end of the hallway, and it felt horrible. It was hard.

But one of the hardest parts of being in Shriners was going to the teen room.

Every patient went to this room at some point, and looking around, it made me realize how lucky I was. Some of these kids were burned on over 90 percent of their bodies and still had to get up and move. I knew how awful I felt trying to move, and I knew I wasn't burned as badly as they were. They had burns on almost every inch of their bodies, and they still had to do the same things I was doing. Some of them had to have skin grafts from their head for other parts of their bodies that were burned. I'd only had my head shaved.

There was a girl, who, I could tell, didn't want to be there. I didn't want to be there, either. So I talked to her, but she wouldn't talk to me. She wouldn't look at me. She wouldn't even say, "Hi." She was miserable. She didn't want to be around people. She just wanted to be alone.

It put everything into perspective to see all of those kids. I thought that I was bad, but when I saw everyone, I knew they had it worse. And I couldn't help them. I couldn't make them feel better.

It made me feel pretty lucky, but sad at the same time.

Never Staying Down

My last week in Shriners, my therapist had me go to the gym for a test. I had to prove I was ready to go home, that I could do some simple things—little things that people do every day and take for granted. I had to throw a ball into a basket two feet in front of me. I had to throw a bouncy ball at a trampoline and catch it. I had to pick things up from off the ground. I had to sit down on a chair and stand back up.

Next, the therapist made me get down to the ground.

I told her I didn't know how I was going to do it because my knee still had a donor-site bandage over it and I couldn't bend it well. I could only bend one knee, and that was limited, too.

She said, "You can do this. I'll catch you."

She was pregnant, and I didn't want to hurt her. But she kept reassuring me. "It's OK. I'll help you."

I stood up. I bent down and slowly got to my one knee, the one I could somewhat bend. I fell over and straight down.

It didn't hurt, it just scared me. I wasn't expecting to fall. I cried, but it wasn't because it was painful. It was because I couldn't believe that I'd fallen. Did that really just happen?

"I Just Want to Go Home"

Another requirement before I could go home was going on an "outing" to make me more comfortable in public.

I had to pick a place to go. I picked the mall because I like shopping.

My nurse went with me. She had prepared me beforehand and asked me what I would say to someone if they stopped me and asked what happened to me.

"Why are you wearing those? Why are you walking like that? Why do you look like that?"

She made me prepare answers.

No one asked me anything, but there were curious stares. I was surprised no one said anything to me.

The mall was packed, and I was walking really slowly. It was still uncomfortable to walk for that long, and it was a mall, so there weren't a lot of places to sit down and rest unless you were getting food. It felt like a whole day, but it was only three hours.

I'd thought I was ready. The outing made me realize maybe I should be a little more nervous about going home.

Lori:

Kilee started getting her sense of humor back as she was being titrated off all medications and was looking forward to being released from the hospital.

Her feet were so swollen that she didn't have any shoes that fit, so we were going to buy her some in the mall. The hospital provided her with medical shoes, and they were pretty funny looking. They were navy blue, open-toed, one-size-fits-all canvas shoes, with thick, white plastic soles and Velcro straps.

We helped her put them on, and she laughed at how ridiculous they looked. They were hideous, but she wanted to go home so badly that she wore them. We teased her and called them her Jordans, which made her laugh even harder. It was the first time she had really laughed since the accident.

She walked into the mall on her own, noticeably dressed with medical garments on her hands and arms. Stares and double takes were predictable, but Kilee shrugged them off with one goal in mind, or maybe two: shoes and home.

The first store we went in, we bought a pair of moccasins that were two sizes bigger than her normal size.

Before going home, she had to be able to brush her teeth, dress herself, get on the ground and back up, go to the bathroom, bathe herself, feed herself, and hold a cup. She also had to completely wean herself off her medication. Plus, she had to continue her therapy, which was getting a lot easier as she healed.

When we left Shriners, Jason gave an update on Kilee's condition on CaringBridge:

December 17, 2014
10:24 PM

I would like to take a moment to thank everyone for all the love, support, prayers, well wishes, visits, and concern for our family and Kilee. This was a tragic accident that has changed Kilee's life and ours forever. It is hard to believe all the support we have received from the community. If we could, we would thank each and every one of you. Just know we do thank you and appreciate the support.

Kilee is scheduled to be discharged from the hospital by the end of this week. That doesn't mean she still won't have a long road ahead of her, but at least she can be at home. Kilee will still come to Shriners three times a week for clinic and physical therapy. She has come a long way since November 10. We could not be more proud of her. She is strong beyond strong. All the progress she has made is a credit to the drive and character she has. Kilee wants her life back and is determined to get there!

We have all been through a lot while here. It's an experience none of us would have ever dreamed would happen. However, the care, understanding, and support we have received at Shriners Hospital has been second to none. We are thankful there is such a place nearby that is dedicated to helping children.

Kilee went home from Shriners a week earlier than expected, on December 18, 2014.

As soon as she was released, she said to me, "I don't understand people who feel sorry for themselves instead of doing something about it; making a change, making a difference. I'm not going to be that person. I'm not going to sit around and feel sorry for myself; I'm going to do something about it."

Kilee:

Driving past my house on our way home from Shriners made me very nervous. But I had to do it. It was across the street from the rental house we moved to after the fire.

With my mom, stepdad, dad, and brother in the car with me, I glanced over to see the old house. It was the first time I had seen it because no one would show me pictures. It was weird to see it like that.

That was what I was in? That was what I survived? I was stunned by how it looked.

Once I saw the house, I started to get a better handle on what had happened to me, and I wanted to see more. I wanted to go inside to see what I had run out of. I was curious to see what was left and what wasn't.

It made me feel sad; we had lived there for so long, and it was Wade's childhood home. But I made it out and I'm OK. Whatever sadness there was, I realized that material things, even important ones, do not matter. I'm here. I'm fine. Everyone is still alive. Everyone is OK.

Then I was OK. I knew we were all going to be OK.

When I got home, it felt pretty good. I hadn't been anywhere, especially a house, in so long. I was nervous because it was a new house and I had never seen it.

I stayed the first night with my dad. I think my mom wanted me to stay with her, but I just wasn't comfortable in a new house yet. She told me if I needed anything that she would come to my dad's house, so that made me feel better.

It was weird to not be in the hospital. There, I had a routine. When I got home, I knew I needed to stretch three times a day, but that was really the only routine that I had other than taking a shower differently.

I didn't have to get up at 7:30. I didn't have to see any doctors. I didn't have to tell anyone what I'd had to eat all day long. I knew I'd rather be home than in the hospital.

Baskets for Brookbank

All my friends were texting me. They were texting my mom. And having their moms text my mom. They just wanted to see me. "When can we come over?"

Some of my friends came over that first week I was home. But I didn't want a bunch of people to know I was home. I told my friends not to tell anyone. "No one can know," I told them.

That week, there was a basketball game between my school and Georgetown, Cameron's school. Every bit of money they made that night was going to be donated to me, an event they called "Baskets for Brookbank." Since no one knew I was home, no one knew I was going to the game.

Everyone was surprised when I got there. People kept looking and smiling and saying hi, asking how I was doing. It made me feel special and loved by the whole community. I could tell that everyone was surprised I was home and had made it to the game. My whole family was there: my grandma and grandpa, my mom and step-dad, my dad and stepmom, my brother, aunts, uncles, and cousins.

Before the game started, I was sitting down with my family, and the announcers told everyone I was out of the hospital and in the school. They made me stand up in front of everyone, and everyone stood up and started clapping for me. It was nice, but also embarrassing. I don't like that much attention.

Even though I was mortified, it felt good to have an entire community supporting me. I never thought that many people would come together for just one person.

While I was in the hospital, they had sent money, cards, flowers, and gifts. It was great to know that many people cared. It felt strange that people were sending money, but the generosity was nice. They felt the need to help in whatever way they could or knew how.

The cards filled up an entire wall. And there were posters, stuffed animals, blankets. One little girl, six or seven years old, whom I barely know, gave me one of her favorite baby dolls. She said I needed her more than she did. I thought it was sweet.

At the game, all my friends were surrounding me, and that was nice—but at the same time, they seemed afraid to touch me or say anything around me. I wanted to say to them, "Hey, I'm still me. I'm still Kilee."

Therapy at Home

I thought it was hard in Shriners, but when I went home, I had to go back for therapy every week. They would give me something new to do from home.

I felt like I'd been doing this stuff for way too long. I just wanted to be able to sit down and relax for two seconds. They made me sit on the ground or crawl across the floor. It was little things like that that they made me do, but I didn't want to do them. It was hard. It hurt. I resisted doing it every time.

I got mad at my mom because she made me do all the therapy I dreaded doing—all the time. She was always telling me I had to do this or that. I didn't want to do it anymore—I thought I'd be done when I left Shriners.

But it was really just the beginning.

I did ten to fifteen exercises at home every day, and they started as soon as I got home. The first week I was home, my therapist told me I needed to try to get onto the floor and get back up. Down. Up. Down. Up.

My mom was standing next to me. I still wasn't strong enough to use my hands and arms to get to the floor. I used the table beside me and leaned on it. I got on one knee and then the other. I was getting down to the floor pretty easily by now, but getting back up was still hard.

My mom refused to help me and told me I didn't need her help. It made me mad and confused because she'd always helped me in life and at Shriners. *Why won't she help me now? Why not just one more time?* I never thought she wouldn't help me. I figured she always would.

But she told me I could do this on my own. And I did. I used the table to gradually pull myself back up. It felt really good. I had so much help for so long, it was nice to be able to do something on my own.

After I fell that day at Shriners, I worried that I would never be able to get up off the ground, or down to the ground. Opening Christmas presents meant sitting on the floor. And it was December, so I wanted to be able to sit on the floor like I did every other year, with Cameron, and open presents from under the tree.

Once I got further into my recovery and therapy, Shriners recommended I try sports medicine therapy. I did that three times a week, every week. They, too, sent me home with stretches to do on my own. They gave me large rubber bands for my legs. I had to lift my legs in the air with them, stretching and pulling.

That's when stretching got a lot harder. It wasn't just sitting in a chair and stretching my hands and arms. This was for my legs. They made me do pushups and sit-ups and planks. It was even harder than all the "impossible" things I had done so far.

But I knew I had to do it.

Lori:

When we got home, we still had to be careful about touching Kilee. We couldn't hug her. The skin grafts on her calves were in terrible shape and she still struggled a little with walking. We knew, however, that walking would come. She had to walk every day to get from point A to point B, so she would get practice. The walking would come.

Our ultimate goal was getting her hands back into shape. After initially being told that she might not keep her fingertips, we wanted to make sure that since she got to keep them, she could use them just as she always had. The other issue was operating her hands. When she came home, she could only close her hands into a partial fist, but not all the way. That was thirty-four days after being grafted.

They had told us she would probably need more skin grafts and have to be cut open again if her skin was not able to stretch the way it needed to for mobility. We hated to hear that; there was no way she could go through all that again. No way could she go through that pain again. It wasn't just the burns, it was the pain after. She was in a lot of pain, even when just picking up a cup.

Her left hand was doing well, but her right hand wasn't. And she uses her right hand the most. However, at this point, Kilee was even texting again—slowly. She was doing everything slowly.

She was up to ten pushups; however, they didn't look much like a pushup. We all laughed. She laughed, too. Kilee was back to her goofy self. We got on the floor with her and did her exercises. We encouraged her and laughed with her. I think it got her back to feeling some sort of normality. She wasn't alone, and she had people who loved her and would be there with her to do everything, including her almost-pushups.

A Christmas Blessing

Thanksgiving was spent inside Shriners with about fifty family members. We all gave thanks for Kilee's escape from the explosion and her speedy but ongoing recovery. But now we felt blessed that she was home in time for Christmas and that our family was together.

Again, Jason took to CaringBridge to share a final update with the community.

December 25, 2014
5:48 AM

Merry Christmas, everyone! I haven't updated this page for a while now so I thought I would fill everyone in. Kilee was released from the hospital last Thursday. She is now home and doing great. She flashes that beautiful smile all the time.

In order for Kilee to leave the hospital, she had to accomplish certain goals set by the doctors and staff. She did those all on her own. By doing so, she was able to leave sooner than first anticipated. Kilee really wanted to be home with family and friends, so she used that as her motivation.

She is healing well. Her mobility gets better every day. We are still required to visit the hospital three times a week for clinic and physical therapy. This is her first week of both, and she has done well. The doctor liked what he saw, and the PT staff is pleased with her progress. Physical Therapy does want her to concentrate on her hands, wrists, and left shoulder.

Thank you to everyone for the support and kind words. We look forward to Kilee's continued recovery in 2015. One of her goals is to be ready for soccer this coming year. So we have a lot of work ahead of us. I know she can do it! Merry Christmas and Happy New Year!

᪥᪥

Kilee:

My favorite holiday has always been Christmas. You get to see your families, give gifts, and I love wintertime. I have always loved waking up on Christmas morning and seeing snow. It is my favorite time of the year, and last year it was definitely my favorite part of the year.

Christmas in 2014 was the best Christmas ever for my family and me. We didn't really know if I would be home for Christmas, but I didn't want to spend my Christmas in the hospital. I worked really hard, and it paid off. I got to spend Christmas with my family like I had every year before.

I spent half of it with my mom and her side of the family and the other half with my dad and his side. It felt just like normal for all of us.

I went to a friend's house for New Year's Eve and got to see a lot of my friends. I was ringing in the new year with a new outlook and a wish.

I was looking forward to how my life would be at the end of the coming year. I couldn't wait until all the therapy was done, and I was excited to see what it would be like to not have to do that stuff all of the time. I could be normal again.

Up Close: I Survived

My family didn't want to take me inside our old house where the explosion happened because they didn't think I would want to or that I could handle it.

But after I asked my mom and told her I thought it could help me a little bit, she agreed. My mom, Wade, and Cameron had been in the house only one or two times, and the only reason they went again was because they wanted to be with me when I went through. Wade only went in once and didn't go back; it was too hard on him.

It was still difficult to grip anything, so when I got to the door, I needed some help opening it. As I walked through the super-charred rubble, the first thing I saw was the living room. The couch and the loveseat were gone, along with the TV, tables, and recliner. There was nothing left but a few remnants of the furniture. Then I saw the kitchen; it was completely gone. You could barely even tell that the cabinets had been there. The table and chairs were gone, and after I saw that, I went to the bathroom. I was in the bathroom when everything happened, so it was one of the places I really wanted to see. When I walked in, I noticed the floor was still there. You could still see the tile with barely any ashes on it. That was where everything started and happened, so I was expecting that to be the worst place in the whole house. Turns out, it was one of the best places.

Walking through what used to be my home, I just kept thinking to myself how lucky I was and how grateful I am for everything. My eyes were truly wide open now, and I knew I had to keep pushing to get to my goal: full recovery from this house and that day.

Bathing Beauty

Even though I was home, I still had to wear a pressure suit to reduce my scarring. It covered my entire body. It made it hard to wear regular clothes—that was another hard part about all of this.

I didn't have to wear pressure garments in the hospital. They just wrapped me up. So once I was home, I had to get used to wearing them.

For the first couple of weeks, I still used the Ace bandages. They were uncomfortable and always fell off of me. Eventually, they had garments made for me and I was able to wear them instead of the bandages.

When I wore the bandages, I could wear a sweatshirt over them and it would show a little on my neck. But with the garments and the vest, it was choking me all the time. It was almost a turtleneck. It was nothing I would choose to wear for looks.

Nighttime was the worst.

I always had to get ready for bed at 8:30. That's really early to get ready for bed, but it took an hour and a half just to get ready and then go to bed. My mom or dad, depending on who I was staying with that day, would rub lotion on me. That part felt good. But no one wants to sit there for an hour and a half every single day, every single night. Plus, to have your parents bathe you when you are sixteen is very weird.

When I woke up in the morning, I had to start all over.

I couldn't move my arms very well, so someone would have to help dress me and fix my hair. I never did that stuff on my own in the garments, because everything was stiff inside them. Plus, once I put the garments on, I couldn't get them wet. It was difficult to do anything that involved water once I put my garments on. I needed help brushing my teeth. I needed a cup to rinse. I couldn't put anything on my hands to fix my hair.

After a few weeks, I was ready to stop using my garments altogether.

~∽∾~

Lori:

Baths were finally down to once a day. Eventually, when I was stretching Kilee's hands at nighttime, I got to the point of saying, "Kilee, you have to do this..."

The doctor had told us we would have to get tough with her. We couldn't baby her. And we didn't. It sunk in that first week of doing stretches with her. We never looked back.

She would get angry with me, and I would love on her and tell her that it's OK if she gets mad, but she was going to have to do this if she wanted to get better. She would agree, and we would go on.

It happened more and more as she realized she couldn't do all of the things her friends were doing. She was a junior in high school and wasn't able to go out with her friends. She knew she had to be home at a certain time because she didn't want to make us more tired by having to stay up later to get her ready for bed—like her massaging, which had to be done every night. At this point, she had so much going on, so many bandages, so much wrapping, that it was a constant struggle and would take hours for her to take her nighttime bath. Jason or I would wash her, all of her, every day. She gradually started doing more and more on her own. I think it was that gradual process that helped her to get back to using her hands and doing all the things she could do on her own before.

Even when she got used to the massaging and lotion after baths, it was still awkward for her to have her mom and dad bathe her and rub lotion on her. There she was, a teenager, and her dad had to see her like that.

From the beginning, she was ready for it to be over. But we had to massage her up to the one-year mark. We always kept it in the back of our minds that it was all just temporary. Any discomfort, pain, and embarrassment—all of it was temporary.

Kilee:

I had skin grafts taken twice from donor sites on my back. And because of that, it blistered and scabbed badly, and was the most painful thing about my whole experience. I didn't like taking showers. Just the water touching me hurt.

There were huge blisters and then they scabbed. I couldn't pick the scabs, because as much as they hurt, I had to leave them on so that the skin would heal. It felt like how a blister in your mouth hurts, times a thousand, and all over. Nothing helped. There was no magic ointment. Lotion made it even worse—it was goopy, slimy, and thick.

There were scabs everywhere; they would always get caught on my gauze and wraps. Every time I moved a certain way it would catch on to something and I couldn't do anything about it. I either had to rip it off and have the scab come with it, or leave it stuck and eventually let it rip itself off. I slept on my stomach with my blanket halfway covering my body, my back exposed, and with the fan on in my room so I could give it some air. I wanted to air it out and hopefully get it to dry out to a point where it would heal on its own. There would always be a lot of liquid that would come out of the scabs and blisters. It felt like something was constantly stuck on my back, like it was chapped, and I could feel it crack. When the scabs finally started to heal and could come off, my dad would try to rub lotion around them and get them to loosen up until they would fall off. By that time, it wasn't as painful as it was before, and it felt good to finally get that stuff off. It felt like my back could breathe again.

Therapy at Shriners

Therapy at Shriners was tough.

Every week, three times a week, we would have to drive an hour there and an hour back. It started as soon as I was released from the hospital, which was during the Christmas break, and continued after school started, which meant that I missed a bunch of school. It was hard to manage therapy, missing school, and trying to do makeup work and get my homework done on schedule.

I wore sweatpants while doing therapy because it was the only thing that was comfortable with my garments. Sweats were part of my life, as was therapy three times a week at Shriners.

In January, I sat down on a Friday for my last therapy appointment at Shriners for the week. My arms were stiff, and while most teens use their fingers to text twenty friends simultaneously, I was struggling to pick up toothpicks from a table and put them into a small square of white Styrofoam.

For that exercise, a pile of wooden toothpicks was placed on the table like a smaller-scaled version of the game Pick Up Sticks. My therapist was patient and talked to me as she slowly, but purposefully, wrapped my fingertips, which were pushing through my tan glove, around one toothpick at a time, sliding each into the thick Styrofoam. I was holding it steady with my other hand, which was wrapped in purple medical wrap.

After I got fifteen toothpicks pushed into the Styrofoam, my therapist told me to pull each one back out, which was harder than it sounds. They were pushed in hard, and pulling them out took a totally different strength that I just didn't have yet.

After I pulled out all fifteen, I had to hold a red medicine ball with both hands and swing my arms up to one side and then down and up to the other side, never dropping the ball.

For my next exercise, I had to grip a plastic clip, open it and place it onto a wooden bar. It was really hard to do, but as I finally got it on, I was so relieved that I smiled and laughed out loud.

Lori:

There were a few appointments when Kilee didn't have her regular therapist, and the therapist she did have would make Kilee and me nervous about her hand.

"It's just not getting any better. This is not good. She's not progressing. She's behind…"

She said they would have to put her right hand in a cast, and if the cast didn't work, they'd have to do another skin graft on Kilee. And all the pain and therapy would start all over again.

On the way home, I told Kilee she was going to have to do more, and she said, "But Mom, I do it. I do it all. How can I fit any more in my schedule? I don't know what else they want me to do. I'm doing it at my own pace and the way I'm comfortable doing it. I can't do it the way they want me to do it. I'm doing it the way I want to do it."

Kilee sat in the back seat, crying.

We met Kilee's normal therapist and asked her what was going on. If this was really something we needed to be concerned about, then we had to figure it out.

"If she's not progressing, you need to help me and tell me what else we can do."

I told her Kilee was scared to death thinking she might have to have a cast and another skin graft.

The therapist told me she thought Kilee was doing well, but she admitted that Kilee was her first full-time patient at Shriners. She was still learning herself as a physical therapist. She said she would talk to her supervisors to find out how Kilee was progressing.

When we went back the next week, a supervisor looked Kilee over and told us she was doing OK, but needed to do more. They decided they would put her in a Dynasplint. A cast would immobilize her and halt her progression, so that wasn't a good option.

We left that room with a splint and a lot more hope.

I could tell they actually cared for Kilee. Genuinely cared. And for Kilee, from that day on, she had the mentality of, "I'm going to do this."

With every scare, she seemed a bit more motivated to get better.

Kilee left Shriners that day with a smile ear to ear.

Let Freedom Ring

Kilee:

I was scared of getting back to driving because of everything my parents said. They were nervous about it too because I was not as strong as I used to be and my hands couldn't function the same way they did before. I knew that they were right, and that is the reason why I thought I couldn't do it. I hated having to rely on other people to take me places. It made me feel like I was a little kid again, always asking my mom and dad to take me somewhere. There was nothing that I could do alone. I have never felt like that ever in my life. I've never had to ask anyone to help me pull my pants up, put my makeup on.

That is partly why I felt motivated to drive again. And I wanted to prove that I could do it, no matter how scared I was.

Mom and Wade took me to the empty county fairgrounds and told me that I had to drive. I knew that it was coming because they had been talking about making me drive for a couple of weeks. When I got in the driver's seat, it felt just like the first time I drove on the road after getting my permit.

Once I started driving, I realized that it wasn't bad and that I could do it. I felt really good about myself. I was one step closer to being able to drive myself places and not have to rely on other people all the time.

About a month after starting back at school, I was able to drive myself there. The steering wheel in my hands felt like freedom. It felt like me. I gained a piece of my independence back. I could do it.

CHAPTER SIX

Bright Spotlight

Lori:

I was cautious in the beginning about letting Kilee talk to the media, but I quickly realized they were sincere, really cared about her recovery, and thought that her story could inspire others. She is recognized in public, and our once-private life isn't private anymore. It has been quite an adjustment.

I've seen Kilee grow and take on more than I ever imagined she could handle. The interviews, stories, posts, messages on TV and the Internet—she embraced it all. She just wanted to get her story out there to help others. From the earliest photos released from Shriners to the media coverage and the fundraisers she has hosted, it's been all smiles. Her personality shined, even after everything she had been through.

Burn Survivor, Not Victim

Kilee:

I am not a victim. I am a survivor.

When I think of a victim, I think of someone who just lets something happen to them and lets it define them. When I think of a survivor, I think of someone who turns things around and doesn't let it define them. I think of someone who makes the best of it.

I don't like it when people call me—or any other person that is in the same situation as me—a burn victim. It sounds like we are allowing what happened to define us. I am not defined by what happened; I'm defined by what I make of my situation.

Media Invasion

Lori:

Seeing online videos and news reports still takes me back to that day.

Going around the curve on Main Street, from that hill, I could see the smoke from Free Soil Road.

People were calling and texting me, thinking it was me that was hurt. Someone messaged me: "Lori, are you OK?"

Then I got a message that said: "Oh, I'm sorry. Is Kilee OK? I just saw it on the news."

I looked at Wade when I got that message because we were still driving to the hospital. I said, "It's already on the news!" And he said, "You're kidding me!"

It was first reported that it was a woman in the house. I looked at Wade and said, "I wish it was me." He just grabbed my hand.

When we got to the hospital, the media was everywhere outside. The media director at Shriners came to me later that night and said their phones were ringing off the hook and they needed to make a statement to the media. She suggested that Shriners put out a statement that Kilee was in the ICU and was stable. That was all we put out there for about a week.

That first week, a bunch of media showed up at Kilee's school. I got nervous because I felt like her privacy was being compromised.

We saw the story on the noon news and then the five o'clock news. There were all these kids talking about Kilee at the school and doing "Kisses for Kilee," selling Hershey's Kisses for a dollar as a fundraiser. I felt like the school should have asked us first. I called the principal and told her I would appreciate it if she would respect our wishes in this until Kilee got better, and to keep the media out of the school. I know now the publicity was in Kilee's best interest, but at the time, I couldn't see it that way.

We hadn't agreed to any of the publicity, but it happened anyway. That's when we realized this was big.

Big. And Kilee's story could help others.

Whenever there is a child involved in a tragedy, it's important to everyone. This was especially important—because Kilee lived. It's a miracle, considering the circumstances.

Local Spotlight on the Journey to Recovery

Three days after the explosion, I received a Facebook message from a reporter at WCPO.com, a local ABC affiliate's website. She wanted to interview us. She had gone the proper route to connect with us; she hadn't just done a story without us or without our permission.

November 13, 2014
7:29 PM
via Facebook

Hi, Lori-

I wanted to reach out to you and offer my deepest condolences to you and your family, especially Kilee. My heart goes out to you. I've been impressed with how our small towns (Georgetown and Ripley) truly rally together. All of the tweets, the fundraising, the prayers, are incredible, and I'd like to help in any way that I can. If there is anything that my family can do, please do not hesitate to ask.

For now, the best way that I know how to help is through my writing and photography, telling Kilee's story, especially on her road to recovery. I am a journalist with WCPO.com, and I would be honored if you would allow me to tell her story over the next few months, get to know you, Kilee, and your family, and allow all those who love and have concern for her to keep up with how she is doing along the way.

Living in Georgetown, I understand our community, but I still am amazed at the outpouring of support that everyone has when someone needs it. I also understand hesitation when it comes to the media, but I can assure you that I will always have your family's best interest at heart in my storytelling. Honestly, I went back and forth about writing you, because, as a mom myself, I did not want to intrude, but I decided that I want everyone to know Kilee's story, because I can tell from her classmates and those at GHS, she is amazing and her story needs to be told.

Thank you for considering allowing me to do this—regardless; my thoughts will continue to be with you and your family.

Truly,
Jessica Noll

ɔ⌇ɕ

Lori:

I talked to Jason about it. While I'm a private person, Jason is even more so. I talked to Wade. I talked to Amy. I let them all read the reporter's message, and they were all in agreement to do a story but to wait until Kilee could be involved. I felt the same way. As long as Kilee was comfortable with it, I was comfortable with it.

We couldn't do the interview in the hospital because Kilee didn't know if she was coming or going, and you never knew her emotional state. She was sad all the time because of the drugs she was on. I wanted her to be completely coherent to talk to the reporter.

Four days later, I decided to reach out to the reporter.

November 16, 2014
11:08 PM
via Facebook

Thank you for your interest in following my daughter's progress. It's been a long and tough week. After much thought, and an overwhelming show of support not only from friends and family but the entire community, we have decided to consider your offer to follow Kilee's recovery. Please contact my husband, Kilee's stepdad, Wade Highlander.

Thanks again!

The first time I met with Jessica at Shriners, I thought, *Wow, she writes fast!*

We felt comfortable with her, and at that point, I wanted to get Kilee's story out. I wanted people to know that it was possible to survive this. With the support of great family and friends, you can get through anything.

Jessica met with Kilee and our family over the next several weeks. She took photos and spent hours with us. She talked to our neighbors, the first responders, and Kilee's doctor and nurses at Shriners. Eventually she came to the rental house we were living in prior to Kilee going back to school, and then she came again with a TV photographer, Lanny Brannock.

I wasn't sure how that would go because Kilee is shy. But Lanny was very nice and, like Jessica, made Kilee feel at ease. She was pretty great in front of the camera. I was shocked. Lanny was shooting a story for the TV station while Jessica was working on a written story for the website. They were sincere and caring, and that's why we felt comfortable with them. They both asked us questions and knew how to pull stuff out of us.

The one thing Kilee did not want was a photo of herself out there. But when Jessica interviewed us over the next couple of months, she took a few photos after some of the interviews once Kilee felt comfortable with her. Jessica reminded Kilee that people wanted to see how far she had come. Jessica told Kilee that if she didn't like the photos, then Jessica would not use them for the story. It was important for Kilee to trust that. Jessica spent all morning with Kilee on her first day back to school—from getting ready at the house to walking into the school for the first time.

That story on WCPO.com meant the world to us. Everything was so accurate and so emotional. Jessica had captured our story well. We all cried while watching it and then reading it. Kilee was a survivor, and that's how Jessica's story portrayed her.

Media Whirlwind

Kilee:

A week or two after I came home from the hospital, my mom told me there were a lot of news people who wanted to do a story with us, but WCPO was the only one she was considering. So she said if I felt comfortable with the reporter, then we could do the story. I told her it was fine with me. From there, it just kept going and more people got involved and interested.

I just assumed that this would be cool and people could see it on the WCPO website and on TV. But then everyone wanted to take the story and put it on their website—big-name people. I didn't expect that. It kind of got old after a while. I was ready to just live my life and leave the spotlight behind.

People knew me before I met them. It was just weird. You could tell they knew who I was. They would look at me but not say anything.

During the first interview at the house, it was strange to have everyone around me, listening to everything I was saying. I wasn't comfortable talking about everything around them.

I thought that if I talked about it, everyone would start crying.

When Jessica came to my house the first day back to school, I was excited. I wanted someone to see everything I had to go through in the morning to get to school.

But once the segment aired, it was weird to see myself on TV. You don't think you sound like that or look like that. There had been a lot of TV stories without me in them, but I had never watched something so true about what had happened to me.

Truth be told, it was super weird to be in the public eye for the first time.

I didn't know what to expect after working with the WCPO-TV and WCPO.com reporter. I knew it would be a different experience; I just wasn't sure what it would lead to or if it would even be anything big. After it was published, I saw it everywhere on my newsfeed on Facebook. It was weird to scroll through my newsfeed and see myself on everything because of how many people shared it. I wasn't sure how to feel about it. I enjoyed it, but at the same time, I wasn't sure what would happen next.

After the WCPO story, a woman with two teenage daughters was the first person to say something to me. Her daughters were staring.

They said something to their mom, who looked at me and said, "Are you that Kilee girl from Georgetown?"

"Yeah, I am."

"Bless your soul. You're such a lucky girl."

She was really sweet about it. I think most people are too scared to say anything. I think I would be, too, if I were someone else. They look and they know, but they don't want to ask. It would be OK if they did. I wouldn't mind telling them what happened. I would kind of feel like it's OK; I would want to know what happened if I saw someone like me walking around. I wouldn't be offended by it; people are curious.

I would tell them: "I lit a candle and my house exploded. I went to the hospital for thirty-eight days and had skin grafts, and that's why my skin looks like this."

Going National

My story started to spread to other websites, such as *Daily Mail* and *Life & Style Weekly* magazine, which posted their own stories based off WCPO.com's article. And then, a producer from *The Doctors* messaged me on Facebook. They must have looked through my page to see who my friends were, and they messaged one of my friends about me being on their show within the next week. I was with my dad, and he didn't know whether to trust it since it was through Facebook. My mom decided to call the number from the Facebook message just to see who it was and what they wanted. At first, I thought it would be cool to go to LA, but I wasn't sure I wanted to be on a TV show that a bunch of people watch all over the world.

That night, the producer called my mom, and he seemed really nice. Everything seemed real, not like we were being scammed. I thought, *What could it hurt?*

The guy from the show called us over the next few days and asked me questions so they knew what to talk to me about on the show. He told us he wanted to fly us out as soon as possible.

Two days later, we left for LA.

Lori:

It was all overwhelming.

When *The Doctors* reached out to us, I kept thinking, *This isn't real.* I had never even heard of *The Doctors*. Kilee was still not 100 percent. Really, I hoped she would just say no to the interview. I was worried about her showers—showers took a few hours. She had to have medication put all over her and then be wrapped up in an Ace bandage. Flying for four hours to LA also gave me pause. But Kilee was insistent. She wanted to tell her story.

I didn't even believe it was real, so I told her I'd do some research first to see if it was legit. I called the guy who reached out to Kilee's friend on Facebook, and my Internet search showed that Dr. Phil was the executive producer of the show.

I spoke to the producer on the phone, and he seemed sincere. They wanted to get Kilee to Los Angeles that week.

Cameron had a basketball game and I didn't want to miss it, so I knew he was the one I needed to talk to. If all the family went and he stayed back, how would he feel? He was upset. He wanted to go too, but he didn't want to miss basketball. I told him Kilee really wanted to go and that I felt that doing that show would help in her recovery. He agreed and told me we should go ahead. Jason said there was no way he could take any more time off work, so he stayed with Cameron.

The show sent a photographer from Michigan to interview us on Tuesday at my office. It was really emotional for me. It was like reliving it all over again. Then he interviewed our neighbors, Stanley and Carol, at their house.

Our flight was early Wednesday morning, January 28. When we got to LA, I looked around, thinking how cool it was. The weather was perfect, dry, and awesome. Kilee did not stop smiling. She loved it.

It was a bright spot in a hard week. She was dealing with a lot, and some uncertainty as well.

She was exercising several times a day, and we were told she might need another surgery if her arms and hands didn't loosen up.

Her therapist at Shriners put her hands in this wax treatment to loosen the muscles. Kilee still couldn't squeeze her hands closed. They told us to keep doing the exercises and stretches. If they didn't see improvement in a week, we would have to re-evaluate.

When we got back from Los Angeles, they had custom-made splints for Kilee's hands and arms that helped her stay stabilized. She wore them all night long, laying on her stomach with her arms out, shaped like a T. She wasn't able to stretch her arms over her head, so sleeping like that helped her to be able to do that.

The possibility scared me. It scared Kilee. It was hard to get her motivated. She was overwhelmed. But the trip to LA got her energized and really changed her attitude about the entire situation. It got her to see what she could do.

City of Angels

Kilee:

Flying was miserable.

My back had a lot of sores. Sitting on a plane for four hours, my butt still sore from burns—just painful. Toward the end of the plane ride, I couldn't sit still anymore. I was itchy and kept getting hot. I couldn't wait to get off the airplane. It was the most uncomfortable thing ever.

I had never been anywhere like LA, so I didn't know what to expect. It was weird with the time difference, and I got tired. The city was cool, though. I think I'd go back, but I'm not sure I'd want to stay there forever.

The show had someone at the airport to pick us up, take us to the hotel, and get us settled. Our hotel was right on Hollywood Boulevard. It was kind of cool.

That night, we went out for dinner, looked at the stars on the Hollywood Walk of Fame, and did a little shopping.

I needed clothes to wear on the show because I didn't have any nice clothes that were comfortable with my scars and fit over my garments. It was only a month after I had come home from Shriners, and I was still uncomfortable.

The next day, a van picked us up to go film the show. We were there from about ten in the morning until three in the afternoon. It felt like forever. We'd bought Lakers tickets for that night, so I was looking forward to that. They were really good seats and pretty expensive.

There were a lot of people backstage. Wade was called into the makeup chair…one minute later, he was back with powder covering his face. Mom and I were laughing.

I got my makeup done while my mom got her hair done. The lady there had done hair for a lot of celebrities. She said, "Yeah, I do this a lot with celebrity teenagers."

I thought, *That's so cool!* If someone did that for me every day, I wouldn't complain at all. They were really good. They knew just what to do. My hair was still super short and I didn't even know how to fix it; somehow they made it look really nice. I said, "Oh my gosh. Come do this for me every day!"

We went back to get dressed. They tell you what to wear. You can't wear white, patterns, or stripes. We asked, "So what can we wear?"

The wardrobe people came in and told us they had things for us to wear if we didn't have something. So they had me put on black pants, which were kind of tight, with a blue shirt. The shirt came down low, and I was wearing my vest over my scars. I told them I couldn't wear the shirt because the vest would show and it wouldn't look good. They said, "Oh, don't worry."

They sent in a lady with a bunch of tape to tape up my shirt. She taped it way up. She also taped the microphone onto me.

Then they made me put on ugly shoes because the shoes I'd brought didn't match the clothes they made me wear. I kept asking, "Are they going to see these on TV? I really hope not."

Then we waited.

National Spotlight Hits

Lori:

We arrived at Paramount Studios and the producers were awesome. They told us what they wanted us to talk about and to stay on script about what they wanted us to say.

I was nervous, hoping Kilee was OK. She looked good. She was really pretty after wardrobe, makeup, and hair. Her hair was really short, but she liked what they did. She had been getting acne for the first time—a side effect from her burns. She had been a little paranoid and didn't really wear much makeup since the accident. So they put some on her and it looked great.

Kilee had a teacher with her the entire day. California law requires you to have a teacher with you if you're under eighteen and doing a show. This lady was a teacher for the

Modern Family and *Black-ish* casts. She was telling us everybody she has taught.

Before we walked out to the stage, they put us in another room. The teacher looked at Kilee and said, "Do you have anyone who you idolize?"

Kilee said, "No, not really."

I said, "Oh, come on, Kilee. Yeah, you do."

"Well, I do like *Pretty Little Liars,*" she admitted.

"You like Justin Bieber; don't lie about it," I joked with her.

"Yeah, I do," Kilee said, all shy. The truth was, she was a huge fan of his.

I looked at the teacher and said: "If that kid could keep himself out of trouble, he'd be all right. I hope he turns his image around. He's in the spotlight so much. I feel bad for the kid."

◈

Kilee:

Some guy took us down a hall and told us to stand by these two stairs and wait. We had our microphones on, so we figured it would be any minute now. Mom and Wade were introduced as the show started; they had me walk out after the show had begun.

When they said, "Come on out here," I walked out onto the stage. On TV, it looked like there were a ton of people in the audience, but there were maybe one hundred, not even that. I was kind of surprised.

I sat down where they told me to sit.

They asked me a few questions and told me how good I looked. Before I came out on stage, they had shown a video about my story with pictures from my recovery and my burns.

They asked me to walk them through what happened to me, as briefly as possible. So I tried to, but it still took me a minute or two to get it all out. They didn't ask me anything else. They just said how awesome it was that I was there, and the audience started clapping.

Then they turned to me and said, "Well, we've got something for you because we know who you like."

I was looking at them like, "OK, I have no idea what you're talking about."

They must have done some good research. I don't know how anyone would've known about me liking Justin Bieber unless they'd gone on Twitter.

While I was at Shriners, some people at my school had tweeted #KileeMeetJB and stuff like that because they knew what a big "Belieber" I was—and had been since the sixth grade. But I was still surprised the show knew about it. I have liked Justin since I heard his very first song on MTV. I never was crazy obsessed like most of his fans are now, though. I just enjoyed knowing about him, and I have always loved his music. Every time he released a new album or song, I would get it and listen to it over and over again. I liked him and his music. I have always thought he was very cute, too.

They showed me a video of Justin Bieber saying hi to me and saying what an inspiration I was to him. I was shocked. I thought it was awesome.

I was confused about why they didn't ask me any more questions about what happened, but now I know it's because that time went to having Justin surprise me. I'm not complaining.

After the video, Dr. Travis looked at me and asked me how the video made me feel.

I said: "It's awesome. I never thought that would happen."

He kept trying to ask me questions, and then the crowd started clapping again.

I thought, *What? Why is everyone clapping? What the heck is going on?* I was confused and couldn't pay attention to what he was asking me because everyone was cheering.

Lori:

Wade and I walked out and sat down.

They showed the video of what happened that day with our interview that we did with them from home. It was like they were trying to make it look like Kilee was running out of the house in the reenactment. They didn't let me see it until the taping of the show, so I saw it when the rest of the audience saw it. They were going off what we had told them and what Stanley and Carol had told them. Obviously, I hadn't seen what happened that day. Watching the reenactment gave me a queasy feeling. It was a bit overwhelming.

Then they introduced Kilee and she came out. The crowd cheered for her.

I wanted to talk about Shriners and how the care Kilee received was incredible. I wanted to talk about the support of our family and friends and how our small community has come together and really helped us get through this. I wanted to tell them how difficult every day is for Kilee and how people don't see what goes on behind closed doors. They see Kilee all put together with an infectious smile on her face.

Those were on my list of things to say.

They asked me about how badly Kilee was burned, and I talked about how her eyebrows and eyelashes were singed. They kind of interrupted me and started talking directly to Kilee again. I thought surely they'd come back to Wade and me and talk to us again. They had asked Wade one question about recovering and the house and his answer was, "Yes." I was thinking they hadn't given us enough time to say everything we needed to say. This was all swirling around in my head while we were sitting there.

Then they looked at Kilee and said, "We have a very special surprise for you. We have someone who wanted to send you a video message."

The producer had asked me a couple of days prior if there was anyone who had helped Kilee through all of this. I'd told them about our family friend who had been burned as a child and talked to Kilee while she was in Shriners. They asked if she'd be willing to do an interview or a video message to Kilee. Of course she would. She had already helped her twice while in

Shriners, showing Kilee her own scars from donor sites on her body. I gave them her contact information and made sure she was willing. I thought the video was going to be from her. How awesome. That would really make Kilee smile.

To my surprise, it was not.

I looked up at the huge screen behind the stage and it was...Justin Bieber.

Meeting Justin

Kilee:

Justin came up behind me and gave me a big bouquet of flowers and hugged me, and that's when I was really shocked.

I was looking at him, thinking, *Oh my gosh, is this even real? Is this really him?*

It was kind of crazy. That's something a lot of people would love to have happen to them. I was excited it was me. It was cool but kind of weird. You never think any of that will happen.

He kept kissing me on the cheek and hugging me. It was surreal.

❧❧

Lori:

I just thought, *Oh my goodness. It's really him sending her a message.* I thought, *How did he know to do that?*

The doctors kept saying to Kilee, "We know how important it is...how special you are...we have a surprise for you."

The crowd was going nuts, and I could see someone behind me. I thought, *Oh my gosh, is he here? Did they bring him here?* I turned around a little and looked and, "Oh my gosh!"

He had a huge bouquet of pink and purple flowers in his hand and was walking over to Kilee, next to me.

Kilee was excited, and I was excited for her. She was melting. She ate it up. He asked her many times, "Can I kiss you?" And of course, she said, "Yeah!" and put her cheek up to him. She just kept smiling.

I was a little disappointed because we had chosen to go on the show to make people aware of all Kilee had gone through, to talk about her.

But Justin's visit did put a smile on Kilee's face.

It was the one thing that truly had put a smile on her face and made her giggle. She was on cloud nine from that day forward. I really do believe that was what jump-started her full recovery, as quickly as she continued to progress from then on out. It made her want to do it. I know that sounds crazy because he's just a person, but he was her idol and she needed that to get to the next step.

It's amazing how much an idol can mean to a child and help her get through so much.

Hanging with JB

Kilee:

After Justin surprised me on the show, he whispered in my ear that he had a surprise for me backstage. He wanted to take me to his studio to listen to some new music he recently had recorded. So I said, "Yeah! I want to go!"

I kept looking at Wade and my mom, hoping they wouldn't say anything about the Lakers game. I really wanted to go to the studio.

I was really nervous about going to Justin's studio. Mom was telling me all day not to get my hopes up and that he might have something come up. But he invited us, so I was sure he'd be there.

One of his managers, who does his scheduling and sends emails for him, told us she'd give us her number and email. We were supposed to go at seven that night, and she emailed us to tell us Justin had something come up and was running late and to go to the studio at eight instead. Then it was 8:30. It kept getting delayed. I thought it was going to fall through.

She emailed us again and told us we could go to the studio because Justin was on his way. We had already been in the taxi because they'd emailed us the address. We went to the address, which was only a few blocks away from our hotel, but when we got there it looked shady. The outside of the building looked nothing like a studio that Justin Bieber would go to. It was a plain, old building. So we went back to the hotel.

She emailed us and told us, "It's OK, you can go. Justin is at the studio." So we got another taxi and tried the address again. There was a big gate, so we couldn't see inside. There was a speaker box on the outside for us to tell them who we were. Wade told the lady who answered that I was supposed to be there to see Justin. And she let us in.

There were fancy cars everywhere. I could see then why they needed such a big fence.

We went inside and there were people everywhere. One of his bodyguards told us to go upstairs and Justin would be calling us down soon. It was the coolest lounge area I'd ever seen. There were two couches that formed a semicircle, with the backs arching up toward each other. It was like sitting in a dome. The ceiling had different-colored lights and there was a TV in there. We sat there for like an hour.

I think it's the lounge where the bodyguards go to get away because they don't want to sit in the studio the whole time. There was a bodyguard FaceTiming with his kid. It was adorable. After he hung up, he was telling us all about his life and his kid and his move out to LA to work for Justin. It made the time go faster.

Wade was looking at all the people who'd recorded albums there. He thought that was cool.

After an hour or so, someone told us Justin was ready for us. We followed him. There were tons of people in that studio. People in the corners, leaning up against the walls, people sitting on the floor, on the couch, on the chairs. It was packed. I don't know what they were doing. I recognized one of the guys as Justin's best friend because I'd watched Justin's movies.

Justin turned to me and asked me if I wanted to know anything about him. I didn't have any questions to ask, because with someone like him, everyone knows everything about him already—so what else was I going to ask? I didn't want to ask him personal things because that's weird. It got quiet, so Mom and Wade asked him some questions. I just sat there and listened. He kept asking me if I was sure I didn't have anything to ask or say. I said, "I'm sure—I don't have anything."

He kept hugging me and telling me he was sorry but he couldn't stop hugging me. I was completely fine with that. Seriously. After he was all hugged out, he asked if I wanted to hear some of the new songs from his album. I said, "Um, yeah! That's cool!"

He played us at least six songs from his new album. He was really nice. He played us "Where Are You Now?" and as soon as we heard it on the radio months later, we knew it. That was cool.

We didn't end up going to the Lakers game.

I told my friends and family about going to his studio, but I didn't blast it on Twitter, Facebook, or Instagram because I didn't want anyone to take that experience away from me. I wanted this memory just for me.

Lori:

Going to the studio was comforting, but awkward. Justin looked at the people on the couch and told them to get up so we could have a seat. I said, "No, no, no. You stay; we'll stand." But he was insistent on us sitting. He got us bottled waters. He didn't make anyone else go get them.

He kept saying to Kilee, "I just keep looking at you. You're so inspiring. I can't stop hugging you. If I make you uncomfortable, just tell me."

Of course, she was fine with it.

Social Media Sensation:

Kilee Who?

Kilee:

The first question people asked me when I got home wasn't, "How are you?"

Nope.

It was, "What was Justin like?"

Even though the show didn't air until February 5, it was already on social media. And Beliebers went crazy!

Lori:

While Kilee was at Shriners, the community, her class-mates, and even unknown Beliebers were tweeting and retweeting #KileeMeetJB because of her love of him and his music. Everyone who knew her knew it would be a dream come true for her.

Beliebers immediately started following Kilee once Justin Bieber tweeted and posted a photo of them to Instagram from *The Doctors*.

Most were supportive, but some said, "Bitch, I'm gonna kill you!" to Kilee for having a photo with Justin.

Twitter Craziness

Kilee:

I'm a really private person.

Immediately after I met Justin Bieber, not very many people knew. I wasn't allowed to tell anyone since the show was recorded before it aired. The people we did tell knew not to tell anyone. Other people started having their suspicions, but no one knew for sure until after the show aired.

Justin tweeted that he met someone special that day, and I knew it was about me. I retweeted and favorited it. And everyone—like all my friends—were asking me if I'd met Justin Bieber. I told them no and blew it off as though I just liked the tweet. He never directly tweeted my name.

When the episode aired, *The Doctors* tweeted something about Justin Bieber being on the show. It was crazy. Everyone was tweeting me, following me. It was just crazy.

Justin even tweeted something about the show.

I have always been a very shy person, and I still am. The media changed how I am on TV and how comfortable I am, but if I first meet you, I am still very shy. I used to not even be able to be on camera for my digital video class. But now I can do it and feel comfortable. I would say I am still the same. I am still shy around people and only comfortable around certain people.

The most followers on Twitter or Instagram that I ever had was about three hundred. But after everything that happened in November, a lot of people from where I live started following me. Once I was on *The Doctors*, they tweeted, and then Justin tweeted and subtweeted about me. People kept tweeting him, asking him who he was talking about.

His fans figured it out, even though he spelled my name wrong, and these people still knew who I was. I soon had more than three thousand followers, and I didn't even know who they were. Strangers commented on my pictures, like, "You're so pretty" and "You're so lucky to meet Justin Bieber." Just crazy things. They didn't even use their real names. Their names were always something to do with Bieber. It was just crazy. I don't know why they wanted to follow me.

I didn't even have gobs of pictures of Justin and me up, just the one—which got seven thousand likes. And I still only have the one posted. I never really posted a lot on Instagram, and I didn't tweet much either. I would tweet to my soccer people or friends. Some people post their life story, but I've never been like that. Now I'm glad that I didn't, because random strangers would know personal things about me. It's weird that a lot of people wanted to follow me; I didn't feel like there was any reason for them to follow me.

It's an invasion of privacy. Some people think it's cool to have thousands of followers, but to me, it's like, they don't even know who you are. You don't know who they are. I don't want random strangers to see anything I do, so I don't post a lot. They don't want to know who I am; they want to know about Justin Bieber and how to get close to him. They seem to think I'm best friends with him.

Most of the comments were really nice, but there was one that Mom freaked out about. She takes everything seriously. More than one person commented on my picture of Justin and me, "I'll kill you!" or something equally awful. But they do that to anyone who has anything to do with Justin. Mom wanted me to delete the picture. She thought they were going to come find me. But they were just being silly, thinking I was Justin Bieber's new girlfriend or something.

Lori:

I realized, eventually, that someone from his team must have seen all the tweets about Kilee tagged with #KileeMeetJB. Once Kilee was scheduled to appear on *The Doctors*, things fell into place. Whether it was savvy marketing or heartfelt compassion, or both, it was an amazing event. Afterward, he tweeted, "I met somebody inspiring today." I still get emotional when I see that tweet because I know he was talking about Kilee.

Later, Justin posted a picture of him with Kilee on Instagram: "Met this inspiring young lady Kilee! She is so special!"

I'm not an avid user of social media. I've always been very private. Kilee has always been very private. It's just our nature.

But social media can be good.

Before the explosion, we would post little things here and there, mainly sports with the kids. After, it gave me some joy to post things about the family and Kilee, because a lot of people would ask me how she's doing. I used Facebook as a tool to update people on her progress.

Social media after Kilee met Justin Bieber was different.

Some posts that Kilee received concerned me. But once I read through them all and noticed that most were positive and supportive of Kilee, I realized quickly that it was just talk and not a real threat.

It didn't affect Kilee at all. She didn't even think twice about any of the negative comments because the positive superseded the negative. In fact, a nineteen-year-old girl reached out to her. She had been burned when she was younger and told Kilee she would get through it.

As with anything else in the news, the hype eventually died down. But people still "like" the photo of Kilee and Justin. We'll never be totally comfortable in the spotlight, but we're committed to helping others.

Kilee's Jump into a Full Recovery

Meeting Justin Bieber kickstarted Kilee into full-on recovery mode. I will always be grateful to him for that.

She got a push from knowing people looked at her as an inspiration and from meeting someone she idolized. But also, knowing she had such support, even internationally, helped her. It truly did.

The show's story on YouTube has had millions of views. It was exactly what Kilee needed to truly begin to heal, emotionally and mentally.

At the end of the day, all of the media attention was incredible, just to see how inspiring Kilee was to so many people. It was eye-opening to see that she's a fighter and she's going to fight, fight, fight until the end. She's going to make it, regardless of her scars.

CHAPTER SEVEN

Starting Over

Kilee:

When I first got home from the hospital, I would think about how my normal life used to be: Wake up, go to school. Come home, then go to practice. Come back home, watch TV, play with the dogs, watch more TV, eat dinner, take a shower, go to bed. I just thought of a simple, everyday type of normal—being able to do things with my friends. I didn't think of going to the doctor or stretching. Or telling my mom it's time for me to take a shower. I would just think of being able to do things for myself.

Lori:

For me, it would be a string of texting:

Me: "Kilee, you forgot to text me after school."

Me: "Where are you?"

Me: "Kilee, are you home?"

Me: "You're making me worry…"

Kilee: "Oh, oops! I forgot."

That's normal.

Every day of her life, she has forgotten to text me and tell me that she's where she is supposed to be. She is the most forgetful teenager that I've ever encountered. That's Kilee. I'm forgetful, but I have age as a reason. She eats slowly, she takes her time on everything, she's a perfectionist and organized or she can't function right, and she forgets everything.

Next, she would text me and ask when I was coming home, because she was hungry.

Fast-forward thirty-eight days later.

"Mom, I can't drive."

"Mom, can you help me get this door?"

"Mom, can you get this bottle open for me?"

"Mom, can you make my plate for me?"

She had to learn how to do everything again—everything, including texting. It just changed that fast. She would text with one hand, drop it, pick it up, and start again. It was just awful. That was not normal for us. That was not in our routine.

She didn't have anything normal in her life.

She looked at me one day and said, "Mom, everything has changed. I have changed. All of us have changed."

Back to Reality

I was exhausted.

I had lost fifteen pounds, and I was already thin. It was really starting to take a toll on me. When you have people coming up to you and telling you that you need to take care of yourself, you realize how bad it's gotten. It wasn't because I wasn't eating or I was sad. I was just occupied with taking care of Kilee and still being able to be a mom to Cameron and take care of him—and being a wife, although Wade and I put that on the backburner for many, many months. It was hard. It was just very, very hard.

I was encouraging Kilee to get back into a routine, doing what she used to do. Shriners taught us that she would heal faster in a routine. Her routine was the first piece to everything getting back to normal.

But she had her garments covering her from fingers to toes. She couldn't even open a door, and she could barely write.

Kilee going back to school, for me, was like the first day of kindergarten. You're excited that they're going to school, but with some reservations. But I knew she was going to be OK. Her cousin and four really good friends were at school with her in case anything happened. I was OK because of that.

Kilee was excited about it—not about getting up in the morning, but just getting back to what she was used to. It had been more than two months since her last day at school, the day of the accident.

I had talked to the principal, and she had a plan if Kilee needed something or if anything went wrong during the school day. Shriners had spoken to the students at school about what Kilee would look like, and they answered any questions the students had.

I did call the school once that first day. I texted Kilee a few times, and she was fine. That was all I needed to know.

I knew I needed to get back to work at some point, even if it was only for two hours. It was a good feeling when Kilee went back to school. It felt like this was the first day on the road to our recovery.

And we were ready. Kilee was ready.

Kilee:

I didn't want to go back right away after coming home from Shriners. I knew my semester was almost over. I figured I'd finish that semester from home and then go back to school when the next semester started.

I turned in a paper for my pottery class and passed the class. I had two college classes. My digital video teacher let me do a paper to finish out my grade for the semester. I couldn't remember anything. I'd already had a bad day the day of the accident because I'd failed my Spanish test. I didn't want to do any more. I thought if I finished up a few things, I'd be good. My teacher told me I wouldn't have to take a final, just a quiz.

I started back January 21, 2015.

Lori:

While Kilee was home after Shriners, friends helped her with her Spanish to keep her grades up. It was still pretty difficult for her to write because of her garments and ongoing stiffness in her fingers.

But now it was time for her to get back to reality, get back to school, and fight for her grades in person by doing the work and getting back into the groove in the classroom.

Kilee wore a hat to school for the first week because of her shaved head. Her school even declared it hat week so she would feel comfortable. Even with everything going on to add challenges, she was still excited to move forward.

Going back to work, I thought about how I wasn't at home to protect Kilee. When I hear sirens zipping by my office, it takes me back to that day. Every single time. It probably will for the rest of my life. That sound changed my life forever. The odd thing is that it has that connection only when I'm in the office; nowhere else.

First Steps Back

Kilee:

The hardest day back at school for me was the very first day.

I got up at 6 AM. Back to reality, indeed.

No alarm needed. My nerves had the best of me, but the excitement trumped any anxiety I had that morning. It was a big day, and I couldn't wait to see my friends.

It was a tad earlier than I was used to waking up back then. I was spoiled being at home after Shriners. But that morning, it was still dark out when I dragged myself out of bed, flipping off the blanket my classmates had made me. It had my soccer jersey stitched in the middle; it matched my entire bedroom at the rental house, which was full of cards and signs of encouragement and well wishes from my school and the community. Leaning against my wall was a five-foot sign with bold letters reading: "STAY STRONG, KILEE." In the corner was a quote: "From every wound there is a scar, and every scar tells a story. A story that says, I survived."

It made me smile as I got ready to face the day and get a piece of my own normal back.

It was a brisk January morning, but it was unseasonably warm at nearly forty degrees. It had been pretty warm the last day I was at school. *Am I ready for this?* I thought.

Like any other morning since being home, Mom helped me with my stretches. Then I threw on a pink zip-up hoodie and black yoga pants over my tan medical garments. They made me feel protected…sort of. Getting everything on was a process that would've normally taken a minute or two, but that day it took about fifteen minutes. It used to be that picking out what to wear was the hardest and most time-consuming part.

I slipped my cellphone into my hoodie's pocket and carefully pulled a black and gray toboggan over my buzzed-short, sandy brown hair. I took a big sip of orange-flavored water, now a two-hand mission with my garments. I headed to the bathroom to brush my teeth—a task that required patience, to say the least.

I laid my toothbrush onto the edge of the sink and squeezed the toothpaste with both hands onto the bristles. I have to be careful not to get my gloves wet, so I used a plastic cup of water to rinse. I couldn't even do that myself. The cups stuck together, so Mom had to pull them apart and fill it for me.

While I was rinsing my mouth, my mom brought me a few pieces of makeup and put them onto the sink. My mom opened my compact. I picked up the pad laying on top and swiped across the powder a few times and then brought it up to my face. I could see a few blotchy red spots on my face, but I covered them quickly with some powder.

Mom picked up my lavender eye shadow and helped me by brushing it across my closed eyelids. I then planned to finish up with my mascara—no small feat. I picked up the tube, but even with two hands, twisting was a challenge, so again, my mom helped me and loosened the applicator from the tube.

I grabbed the applicator and looked in the mirror. My fingertips peeked out of my tan garments, and that's what I gripped the mascara with as I brushed my eyelashes upward. I gazed intensely into the mirror, and with each swipe, Mom said my eyes grew larger and larger.

With Digger and Doogie at my feet—they never left my side the whole morning—I stood back and glanced at my reflection. Good enough.

My cousin Loren, a senior, pulled into the driveway to pick me up.

It was a challenge to open the car door. I couldn't get my fingers around the handle, so Loren opened it for me.

I threw my pink backpack into the back seat and gently sat down, settling into the front seat of the Mazda. We left with enough time to swing through the McDonald's drive-thru for a quick bite to eat.

I wondered: *Will they stare? Will they treat me differently? Will they understand?*

We arrived at school, and at 7:50 AM it was time to go inside.

The sun was peeking through the clouds. I slowly made my way from the car to the larger-than-life double doors leading into my next step to recovery. As I walked in, I felt like I was walking into a world I remembered one way and a world where everyone remembered me differently.

My uncertainties of change and the fear I had of my friends treating me differently—the fear of stares and whispers—quieted once I stepped inside.

So many people wanted to talk to me, and I couldn't get around very well. It was tough. I had to have my friends help me with everything I did, and I always felt like a bother to them. I hated feeling that way even though I knew they were OK with helping.

Everyone greeted me with smiles; my friends hugged me. Walking down the hallway, I passed "Pray for Kilee" signs that had my school picture and a banner that said, "Welcome back, Kilee!"

It put things into perspective very clearly. It made me realize how much my friends meant to me.

We all gathered into the gym for an assembly. I sat with my friends and Loren. It felt good.

That morning, with my friends, was the first time I had really, really laughed. It wasn't anything that anyone said or did that made me laugh; it was just knowing I was back at school and hanging out with all of my friends again.

It was nice not to be sitting at home. I'd spent so much time with everyone—my mom, my dad, my brother, Wade—and I just wanted to spend some time with my friends and get out of the house and maybe even have some alone time.

At first, I couldn't do anything. I couldn't drive myself. I had to ride with my cousin or have my mom drop me off and pick me up. Normally, I would have gone to eat somewhere after school with my friends, but I couldn't do anything because I couldn't move well enough.

People I wasn't really close to would just look at me, but I knew they were just curious and had good intentions. It made everyone in our school seem closer somehow. It was like everyone realized there is more to life than high school drama.

When I had to write for class, I could, but it looked like a third grader's writing. Plus, it hurt. When I'd go back and read it, I couldn't even read what I'd written. Holding a pen in my hand felt awkward, like I was writing with the wrong hand.

I'm Still Me

Everyone at school wanted to help me in every way they could.

Because I had to wear my garments and my splint, my friends would ask, "Do you need me to write that for you?" And I knew I'd have to tell them no and do it myself so I could get stronger.

I knew they were just trying to be nice. They didn't understand that I wasn't really allowed to have help. I was supposed to do everything on my own, even though I wanted help.

I never really explained it to them, so it was hard. I just told them, "No, I've got it."

I felt like they were treating me differently.

They wanted to help me, but they also left me out of some things, like conversations they had that they thought I might think were stupid or petty because of everything I had gone through. But I just wanted to be treated like me. It made me sad because these were my friends for so long and I just wanted them to treat me like normal. It made me mad, too. I felt like they should know they didn't have to treat me like that.

Eventually, I started to go to eat after school with friends, and it finally started to feel normal. I could be me for a little bit. I didn't have to go straight home to my mom and Wade, who would tell me to stretch.

My mom went back to work, and I was glad. I didn't want to hold her back from doing anything she wanted to do. It felt good once things started to get back to the way they used to be.

Hard Adjustment

Lori:

It was overwhelming for Kilee for the first few months back at school. There were minimal projects she had to do to get caught up, but she had four other classes that semester too.

I called her Spanish teacher, who told me she wasn't going to have Kilee take the final exam she missed from the first semester, only the last test. I told her that was a good idea because Kilee was beginning to get overwhelmed. We never heard anything else about it, until three or four weeks into the second semester. Her teacher stopped Kilee in the hall and told her she still needed to take her final exam and last test. Kilee was upset because she has to be in the room to learn Spanish. She doesn't get it just by opening a book and studying.

I called the principal and she talked to the teacher, who said Kilee could have more time but she needed to turn in the test because the class was for a college credit. Kilee went after school three days a week, on top of therapy, and finally took the test before prom. She bombed the final test. She started with an A in the class and ended up with a 90, which is a B. She was disappointed, but I told her that a 90 would be an A in college.

She got straight A's for the whole second semester.

Constantly Doing Therapy, Everywhere

Kilee:

Shriners gave me stress balls. They had hair on the top and a little smiley face on them. They were hard to dislike, but I managed.

I wanted to throw them at anyone who told me to pick them up and squeeze. I wanted to stomp on them. I had to take them everywhere. And squeeze. I had to take them in the car. And squeeze. I had to take them to school. And squeeze. Then Mom thought I'd need them forever, so she bought me a twenty-four pack of them, so now I have stress balls everywhere. I was trying to be normal, but I had to bring a piece of my therapy with me every single place I went, including school. And squeeze.

I would have to randomly drop everything and do therapy and my stretches. Even if we were out to eat somewhere, my mom would tell me I had to do something.

"You have to move. You have to stretch. You can't just sit there; you'll get stiff."

And I did get stiff if I didn't stretch. But it got old hearing the same thing over and over. I just wanted everyone to stop talking about it. I never wanted to hear the words "stretch" and "therapy" ever again. I didn't want anyone to say anything to me. It was hard because I saw everyone around me being normal. No one had to stretch or move if they didn't want to.

Everyone else could just wake up and go to school. They didn't have to stretch all the time and everywhere.

It got really old sitting in class and watching everyone else sit, relax, write with a pen—while I was over there squeezing on stress balls because I couldn't use my hands the way they could. It was hard to see other people doing normal things. If I hadn't been around them every day, seeing them do what I wished I could have been doing, it wouldn't have been so hard.

The hardest struggle for me through therapy was knowing I was the only person around me doing any of those things. No one I knew was doing therapy at home or going to physical therapy almost every day after school. It was worse when my friends would ask me to do something after school and I had to tell them no because I had to go to therapy.

When I got home from school every day, my exercises awaited me. I only had to do these exercises once a day, but I'd already been at school all day and I just wanted to come home and watch TV. And I knew none of my other friends were going home and working out every night.

It wasn't fair.

My mom would always tell me I couldn't skip therapy because it was what would help me. And because she said that so much, it got annoying to me. We argued a lot. That was probably the hardest struggle through it all, because my mom and I never used to argue that much.

A Whole New Homecoming

Lori:

During one of Kilee's therapy sessions at Shriners, we found out she'd been voted to the homecoming court. The school called me to find out if Kilee was going; they didn't want to announce the homecoming court to the school until they knew.

When I told Kilee, she was surprised that she was on court, and when I asked if she wanted to go, she said, "Well, I can't really tell them no, can I?"

Kilee:

I had decided I wasn't going to homecoming.

But…that changed.

I was voted to the homecoming court, as a junior attendant, before I was even back in school. Loren kept trying to talk me into going. But I knew I wouldn't be able to wear what I wanted, and really, I just didn't want to go. Some girls live for being on homecoming court. I didn't care. But they voted for me, so I decided I should go.

Normally, I'm a really big procrastinator. I never went dress shopping until a few weeks before homecoming. I never did anything on time.

That year was different. I had to go shopping way ahead of time to find a dress that would work with everything I had to wear, with my garments. I couldn't wear just anything I wanted. I had to sit down and think about what I needed instead of just buying what I thought was pretty.

I went with my dad to look at dresses at a store in town. I usually liked their dresses, and we needed to go to town anyway, so we stopped by. There was one dress that looked OK on the rack. My dad picked it out and suggested that we add sleeves to it. I took pictures of it but didn't buy anything that day.

I didn't want that dress. I was holding onto the hope that there was something better, different—different color, different style, a different dress completely. I thought of it as a backup dress. I never thought I'd have to get it until I went shopping with my mom, Amy, and Loren.

The day we went shopping was supposed to be a really fun day. A girls' day looking for dresses. Homecoming dress shopping was something I had always looked forward to in years past.

We went through a few stores, but I didn't find anything I liked that was at all pretty, and the few I liked I couldn't wear because of my garments. Because they covered and protected my scars, I had to wear them.

I was having no luck finding a homecoming dress, and my mom had been on me all day about using my stress balls to stretch my hands. I didn't want to shop anymore. I had to stretch and wear sleeves and do all of this stuff that no one else had to do. I just wanted a normal dress.

I was already frustrated when we got into the car to head home. And then my mom made me sit in the back with her and she stretched my hands. I didn't want to do that. I wanted to be normal. I wanted to be like any other girls looking for a homecoming dress. Everyone around me was having a good time, and I was miserable. I couldn't find a dress. I couldn't just sit and relax. I had to stretch. I had to be doing something all the time. It was really tiring and frustrating.

I sat silently crying as my mom pulled and bent and held my hands and fingers to keep them stretched and limber.

After that shopping trip, I kept trying but it was hard to find something. I even looked online, but most people who get long sleeves usually have the back cut out or something that revealed some skin. I just wanted something that would cover everything.

My dad bought the dress we'd seen together. I really didn't like it, but it was the only one that worked with my garments. But I did get to wear heels. I didn't have to wear tennis shoes for the first time in months. I love wearing heels, always have. They helped me feel like myself.

My homecoming dress was not me. It was long and had a slit. But it was the only thing I could find that covered where I needed it to.

The previous year's homecoming, I got to buy a short dress. All I had to do was buy something that I loved. It was red with nude cutouts and sparkles. I loved it. And my shoes were specially made. They were originally nude heels, but the seamstress took a piece of fabric from my dress, which she shortened, and covered my shoes so they looked like my dress. It matched perfectly. It was really cool.

But it wasn't like that at all this time. Now I had to look for a dress that would cover me. I didn't know what people's reactions would be.

The dress was long and white. It had sequins. At the top, it was like a turtleneck and it pinned in the back. There were these big, gaudy-looking beads all over the nude part up by the neck, choking me the whole time. I could have worn a shorter dress if I didn't mind my garments showing, but my mom and dad thought I'd be more comfortable in something longer.

It was not cute. I could never see myself in something like that. Ever.

We had someone make nude-colored mesh sleeves to cover my garments. But we shouldn't have done it, because it was supposed to look like my skin. But it didn't. It made it look worse.

I had my hair styled a little bit. It was so short that there wasn't much to be done. You couldn't put a straightener through it, let alone a curling iron. I put my makeup on, but I worried about breaking out on my face even more than I already was; acne was a strange side effect to the burns on my face.

I started to get acne really badly after a couple months of being home. I have never had acne, ever! I wasn't used to it. I wanted it to go away, and I was confused because I wasn't sure what caused it.

When I went back to Shriners, I asked them what could have caused it and they told me that sometimes it happens after being burned. They told us I could start using Proactiv, and that's what I did. It worked, thankfully, and I got rid of all of the pimples. Now my face looks the way it used to.

At homecoming, my body was tight. My skin was tight. In pictures, my arms are bent because it was hard for me to straighten them. It didn't hurt, it just felt tight.

The dance itself was not fun. At. All.

I sat in the corner the entire dance, not feeling comfortable. I watched people, but I didn't want to be there so I didn't talk to anyone. I wanted to go home.

ও৶

Lori:

I was proud of her for even going.

She hated it.

I had taken her dress shopping and she hadn't found anything she liked. None of the dresses was for her. It was not fun. And she pouted the whole day.

She was not herself.

And I had to be mean. I had to be the mean one like we were told we would have to be in the hospital. To get anything accomplished, we had to make her do her therapy, so I made her do it. I did not let that bother me but for maybe five seconds, and then my mind would do a reversal.

No, she's going to get better. I will make sure she gets better even if she doesn't want to do it.

She said nasty things to me, which upset Loren, but I knew it was just the situation. It wasn't Kilee. I didn't let it get to me. I pushed forward. I wasn't going to prioritize my feelings over Kilee's healing.

I hugged Kilee and told her I loved her and that this was part of it now if she wanted to make a full recovery. Being like that to her was a big part of her getting through this. If I hadn't been there to be the nagging mom, she wouldn't have been doing a lot of the work.

The next weekend, Jason bought Kilee the dress they'd previously seen, but she wasn't happy with it.

We knew we'd have to have whatever we picked altered with nude-colored mesh sleeves. We couldn't find any long-sleeved dresses and Kilee still had her garments on. We were just trying to accommodate her needs, not necessarily worrying about the prettiness of a dress.

Her dress turned out absolutely beautiful, but Kilee had lost so much weight that she didn't look like herself. Normally, she's an athletic 115 pounds, just a beautiful build. But then, she was barely one hundred pounds. Her breasts were the first thing gone. In fact, when she was in Shriners, one of the first times she looked down while they were bathing her, she looked at me and said, "Where are my boobs?"

She didn't look like the Kilee we knew—from her uncharacteristic acne to her short hair. The last time she had short hair, she was seven years old. She was not used to looking the way she did, and she was visibly uncomfortable.

I've seen her burns, open wounds, and scabs. But on homecoming night, she looked beautiful.

Seeing her like that was a relief. She was still beautiful and she could pull it off. It wasn't the ideal situation, the dress she would have picked, or the hair she'd normally have. I was proud of Kilee for being strong enough to walk out there in front of hundreds of people in the gymnasium. The crowd went nuts when she walked out—nuts. They all stood up, clapping and yelling for her. It was pretty awesome.

Kilee was proud of who she was and didn't worry about what others thought.

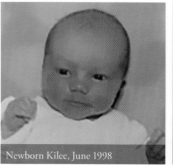
Newborn Kilee, June 1998

Kilee at her 1st birthday party

Cameron, 4, and Kilee, 7, all smiles

Kilee graduates kindergarten, age 5

Kilee before homecoming, February 2014

Together on a girls' day in August 2014

Cameron and Kilee in September 2014

Our home was totally destroyed by the fire.

The photos above are used by permission of WCPO-TV, Cincinnati, Ohio.

Inside, all of our possessions were damaged or lost forever.

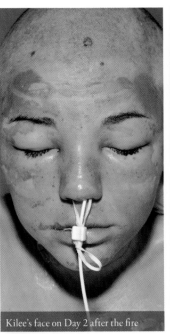

Kilee's face on Day 2 after the fire

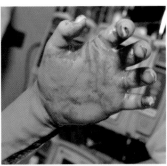

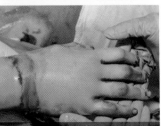

Her hands were burned so badly, Kilee had to relearn simple tasks such as tying her shoes and turning a doorknob.

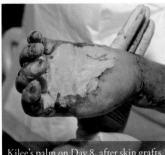

Kilee's palm on Day 8, after skin grafts

Kilee's back was covered in scabs after twice providing skin for grafts on other parts of her injured body.

Kilee on Day 37, the day before she was released

We appeared with Wade (far left) on *The Doctors* in Los Angeles in January 2015, joined by a special guest: Justin Bieber.

Later that night, we were treated to a private visit with Justin in one of his recording studios.

Kilee and Loren before prom 2015

Kilee and her best buddy, Digger

On Homecoming Court, February 2015

Kilee was a bridesmaid in Jason and Brooke's May 2015 wedding.

Kilee with her Shriners doctor, Richard J. Kagan

Kilee in action during her senior soccer season

Teammates Kilee, Kristen, Suzanne, and Lexi

Houstin, Wade (with Doogie), Collin; Kilee, Lori (with Digger), Cameron (with Dori)

Kilee with Loren, her cousin and best friend

With Amy and Loren at Amy's wedding, August 2015

Cousin love, Thanksgiving 2016: Kenton, Loren, Kilee, Avery, Luke, Cameron, and Addy

Two fundraisers, Kisses for Kilee and Baskets for Brookbank, yielded a donation of almost $32,000 to Shriners Hospitals for Children–Cincinnati in 2015.

Kilee, summer 2016

We presented Shriners Cincinnati with proceeds from the 2015 charity golf outing.

Houstin, Collin, Kilee, Alec, and Cameron at the 2016 golf event

Daughter and mom, June 2016

In 2016, Kilee gave Shriners Cincinnati a check for $55,565 raised through the second golf outing.

CHAPTER EIGHT

Big Little Brother

Lori:

I usually pick Cameron up from school. The day of the accident, he texted me and asked if his friend could come over, and I told him that was fine. Not a few minutes had passed before he texted me back and said they were just going to stay at school. I made sure he had some money for a drink and a snack before basketball practice at four.

Staying after school meant Cameron had to go to the library before practice. The school allows kids to go to the library after school to do homework if their practice doesn't start when school gets out at 2:40. Cameron doesn't normally have homework, so he usually writes or draws to pass the time. It seems boring to me, but that's what he chose that afternoon. Thank goodness he wasn't in the house that day, but he doesn't see it that way.

Fast-forward to his basketball practice when the explosion happened just a couple of miles away.

I was outside the house with Kilee, Wade, and Amy. Digger was circling us, barking, and would not leave us alone. Meanwhile, Wade was hugging Kilee, trying to console her because she was freezing. She was practically naked, and there were burn holes all over her pants. As I was standing there, a thought popped into my mind: Someone has to go get Cameron. Someone has got to let Cameron know what's going on.

By that time, I had calmed down because Kilee had told me to chill out. And once I was "calm," I thought of Cameron. I asked Amy to get him, and she did.

I had this feeling of being only partially there for my kids. Kilee and Cameron were always together. I was grateful he wasn't in the house, and at the same time, I was upset that Kilee was. You just feel torn. You want to be there for both of them, and I wasn't there for Cameron right then. It's something I had no control over. He was thirteen and he did not understand. He just did not understand.

Cameron:

We had a routine.

We both got up at 6:30. Kilee would go and get her stuff done in the bathroom, and I'd put in my contacts in my room. After she got done in the bathroom, I'd go in. On the day of the accident, after everything else was done, I put on my Nike socks and my shoes, black and gray Nike Hyperdunks. Everything had to match my Duke shirt and black Nike shorts.

Just like any other Monday morning, it was just "bye" to Kilee as I left.

I got a tired "bye" back from her.

And then Mom took me to school at 7:05.

School got out at 2:27. My friend and I were supposed to go to the house, but we had basketball from four to six. We ended up just staying at school because all our basketball friends talked us into staying instead of going home and waiting. At three o'clock, I asked Mom to go to the house and get my basketball stuff for me.

At 3:30, we walked over to the elementary school gym, got ready, and shot around before our coach got there. We started doing our warm-ups, but around five o'clock, my coach started getting phone calls. All of us were wondering why he was getting so many phone calls. He knew. The assistant coach knew too. But they weren't allowed to tell me because my mom told Aunt Amy to make sure she was the one who told me, not the coaches. Fifteen minutes later, we were doing a shooting drill. I shot and airballed it. I was embarrassed. Someone opened the door, and I looked over. It was Aunt Amy. When I saw her, I could tell she'd been crying. I was thinking, *What is she doing here and why is she crying?*

My coach and the assistant coach walked over to Aunt Amy. Then they called me over. I thought, *Oh, this might not be good.*

I thought maybe I'd done something wrong. My coach hugged me and told me he was really sorry. That put me on my guard.

The assistant coach told me that she was in his prayers. I was confused. Aunt Amy looked at me and said, "Your house is on fire."

"Huh?"

"Your house is on fire."

OK, well, it's just a house. "Is it still on fire? Did everyone get out?"

But they wouldn't tell me anything.

We walked out of the school, and I put my stuff in Aunt Amy's trunk. When we got into the car, I asked her what really happened. She told me about Sis and that she was burned. I was thinking it wasn't major. I mean, I'd burnt myself before on the stove and it wasn't that bad.

It's not that bad, I thought.

Aunt Amy said, "It's bad." I started thinking about Sis and everything that was in the house—every single thing that was valuable that got ruined. While we were driving, I was on my phone and people were texting me that it was on the news. It had only been forty-five minutes since it happened.

I was thinking, *Wait, we're on the news?*

No one told me at all. All I knew was that Kilee got burned and the house was on fire.

We were on our way to the hospital. Aunt Amy was bawling in the front seat; her fiancé was driving. I was in the back seat with my cousins, Luke and Loren.

Before I lost service on my phone while driving through Hamersville, I looked up the news online. I was anxious and typed really fast. I clicked on the live news video, and that's when I saw it—it was a bad way of finding out. My house looked nothing like it did when I'd seen it last.

It was black, smoky, dirty—just really gross. I thought, *Is this really happening? There's no way this is actually happening.*

It was just really bad. My service went out on my phone. I just sat there in the silence. No one talked. The radio was off. It was just sad at that point.

Bad Becomes Real

Lori:

When he first got to the hospital, Cameron was joking and cutting up, and Wade finally had to pull him aside.

"Cameron, it's bad."

"How bad is it?"

"It's bad, Cameron. She could lose her life."

That's when he broke down. He finally realized. He hadn't seen Kilee like we had seen her. He didn't know what to do or what to say, so he was trying to act normal—until he knew it was bad.

I hugged him, but it just wasn't enough. The words "She'll be OK" never came out of my mouth because we just didn't know.

That night, when Cameron was going in to see Kilee, I warned him that she didn't look anything like herself. When he saw her for the first time, he cried.

I said to him, "I know you're the little brother, but you've got to be the big brother now. We need your help. Kilee needs you. We need you."

I think that's when everything was put it into perspective for him, and he started helping us with everything we needed. He helped with anything and everything.

"Cameron, would you go get me a drink? Cameron, would you get a cup of ice? Cameron, would you sit in here with us?"

It took until the last two weeks that Kilee was at Shriners for Cameron to come and sit in the room and interact with all of us. He just couldn't sit still. It was on his mind that much.

Kilee couldn't do anything on her own. She couldn't use the bathroom, nothing. And Cameron saw some of that. Until she was able to get out of bed and walk, it was hard for him to comprehend her getting better.

With her head shaved and her face swollen, Kilee looked a lot like Cameron. They looked like twins.

He walked in and saw her a few weeks into her stay and said, "Mom, she looks like me!"

Cameron:

Luke and I were sitting in the waiting room talking, joking around. No one else was talking. More and more people showed up over the next few hours that I sat there.

Wade looked over at me before I was about to head back to see her, and said: "This is serious. She doesn't look nearly the same as she did before."

A woman with Shriners came out and told us it could be seventy-two to eighty days before she got out. I stopped listening. I was just thinking that's a long time to be in a hospital, and I was hoping she wouldn't miss too much school because of it.

I didn't get to see her until about nine o'clock, and I didn't see her for very long.

She had at least ten medical machines hooked up to her that night. She had four nurses with her because she was in a critical condition. There were nurses running back and forth trying to stop Kilee's pain.

She looked completely different. Her face was pretty big. Her lips weren't the same. Her eyes weren't the same; one was smoky. Her hair wasn't the same. It was shaved. But somehow, her eyebrows weren't much different.

Her toes were sticking out of her bandages. They were the same as I remembered, with paint on them. She was wrapped in bandages. I couldn't see any of her body other than her face, neck, and toes.

She was knocked out, but somehow, when I walked into the room, she woke up. It was slow, but she woke up and saw me. I don't know how, but she smiled at me and said, "Hi."

Then she fell back asleep.

I Am Cam

I'm a junior at Georgetown Junior-Senior High School. I play soccer and basketball. I have a collection of shoes, which I color coordinate. It's kind of weird, but I also have a collection of socks.

I like to build things. Even if it's the hardest thing ever, I'll still try it. When I was little, I used to build with Legos; now I build things like a table, or a TV, or a computer. I think I like the technology side because that's what my dad does; he teaches me that kind of stuff. I remember everything. Anything I do, I remember. I never forget it. My sister is the complete opposite. She remembers nothing unless she writes it down. But remembering everything is definitely a blessing and a curse.

I want to be a sports agent because I like sports, or an architect because I like building and designing. I wanted to go to Duke University, but that's changed because I don't want to be too far from my sister or even my whole family—anyone who is in my everyday life. It would be hard without them. No one at school would compare to my family. If I was far away and something happened, then I couldn't do anything about it. I don't want to not be there again. If I'm closer, I can be there.

Lori:

Jason has always called Kilee "Smiley Kilee," but Cameron smiles more than anyone I know. That kid is always smiling.

Cameron is very loving. Most teenage boys would be standoffish, but he's not. He's very caring and kind. And most of all, he always wants his sister's approval and her attention.

He's a brain and very athletic. They're both smart, but in very different ways. They're athletic, but in very different ways.

One day, Cameron and I were sitting together and I said something about eating like a bird because people always tease me that I don't eat a lot.

He said, "Well, actually, birds eat double their weight." That's the sort of thing Cameron knows.

We were at Norris Lake on the boat, and we were looking out onto the lake with beautiful walls and cliffs around us.

He was sitting next to me, and he looked over at me and said, "Mom, you know why that's uneven?"

"No, but I'm sure you're going to tell me."

"Because something physical happened to it."

"OK, let's talk in my terms. You're saying Mother Nature made it go like this instead of straight?"

"Yep!"

That's just how he is. He's super smart and likes to figure things out. But until the accident, he could never figure out the most complex thing in his life—and that was Kilee.

The Day After

Cameron:

That night, I stayed with Aunt Amy. We got about two hours of sleep and then woke up at 8:30. I packed up for school and got my basketball stuff for team photos. I hadn't seen the house yet, so we drove past it. They wouldn't let me out. All I could see from the window was blackness. I was shocked; I had never seen anything like that before, not in person. I saw stuff on TV and said, "Enh..." But once you see it in real life, off TV, it's a lot worse than on TV.

Aunt Amy dropped me and Luke off at school around ten. That school day was bad. I didn't talk. I didn't eat. I didn't drink. I don't even think I was walking straight. I think it was anxiety and shock still. Even though it was a day later, it was still there—that bad, adrenaline-like feeling.

Sixth period rolled around and we got called to the gym to get our picture taken. We went into the locker rooms to change into our uniforms, and it was about two o'clock before we had our picture taken. It was probably the fakest smile I've ever done. It was hard to make myself smile. I'm standing here, after what happened, and trying to make myself smile after seeing her like that?

I had gotten to the hospital around 7:00 but didn't get to see Kilee until 9:30. I saw her for maybe five minutes; that's it. She looked completely different from when I had seen her that morning at seven o'clock before Mom took me to school. She had short hair, almost bald, and she had needles in her neck and a feeding tube in her nose. They didn't need to give her oxygen. They had tested her lungs and they were perfect. That shocked me. She was in the house for at least a minute and could have breathed in pure smoke.

How's Your Sister?

Lori:

I knew Cameron needed to go to school. I knew he needed to play basketball. He needed to do those things, and we needed to make him do those things to keep him focused and not worried about Kilee.

He barely knew the stuff that went on with Kilee, and we kept it that way intentionally because we did not want him to have to go through those feelings. He was already going through enough.

He missed only five days of school in the thirty-eight days Kilee was at Shriners.

Before this, Cameron had maybe two B's on his report card, ever. His first report card that year, he had straight A's, which was pretty typical. That nine weeks, he had two A's and five B's. I just looked at him and said, "Great job, Cameron!"

I don't know how he managed to do that.

The third nine weeks, I said to him that I understood that he'd had a hard time with Kilee being in the hospital, but she was on the mend and continuing to heal. He had no more excuses. I told Cameron he needed to get back to himself and stay focused on school. I think he got one B on the next report card. I felt like he was back on track.

Cameron:

People came up to me constantly and asked me how my sister was doing. It made me feel like no one really cared about me. They were focused on Kilee. It was about the whole family. We all went through this. It wasn't just about her. And I wasn't doing well.

Everyone at school offered their houses if I needed to stay with any of them. And any time I needed help with something, they'd help me with it. It felt really good to know everyone was there for me, because my parents couldn't be, because they were at Shriners. At times, I felt like everyone wanted to help; at other times, I felt like no one cared about me personally.

My girlfriend at the time was always there. She was always asking me how I was. There is no way I could have kept it together if she hadn't been there. She was always making sure everything was taken care of around me. She left class a few times and brought me my lunch tray because she knew I wouldn't eat otherwise. She'd make me eat. She made sure I was OK while my family was at the hospital.

I had one of my favorite teachers for a class, and every day he made sure I had everything I needed. He was there for me to talk to, you know, guy to guy. We talked about how it still didn't feel real and it was still shocking that it had happened. I talked about how sad I was and how mad I was that it even happened. He asked how I was.

How I was, was feeling like I wanted to punch the wall because there was no one specific thing to be mad at. It just happened. But why did it happen?

For a half an hour every week, from December to the end of the school year, I met with my mentor and my teacher. He wanted me to become a mentor to other students when I got older, so he introduced me to my own mentor who would prepare me to do that.

Every Wednesday we talked about everything: his life experiences, my life experiences, favorite sports teams; anything, really. He was burned on his legs and toes when he was younger. He was about ten years old when he thought blowing stuff up was cool. There was gasoline in a barrel and he lit a match; the barrel tipped over and the gasoline got on his ankles and burned him. He knew what Sis was going through, especially the pain she was feeling.

I opened up to him because he was a guy I could talk to; I wasn't going to talk to my friends about how I felt. It was perfect timing for me to talk to him.

I hope I can mentor other kids, using my life experiences, to help them with their lives.

Shadow of Guilt

The week after the explosion, I felt like I had a hole inside my heart. Kilee wasn't making a lot of progress in the beginning, and she looked awful.

She was just in pure pain. It was hard to hear her scream in the hospital. I had to leave her room and go to the suite. I would lie in the bed and stare at the ceiling and just think about everything. I'd pull myself together and go back to the room once Kilee was done.

One day I told Mom I felt really bad that I hadn't been there to do anything. I told her I couldn't forgive myself. I think it broke Mom's heart when I told her that I felt guilty, because she knew there was nothing anyone could have done. I felt like I should have been there in the house with Kilee to help save her, or even outside the house after the explosion to help her. It felt like I had a hundred-pound weight on my back pulling me down. Nothing felt right. I wasn't sure anything would ever feel right again.

Lori:

During Kilee's first week in the hospital, Cameron's soccer team made it to the state tournament in the Elite Eight.

Kilee, in her drugged-up state, told Cameron she wanted him to get six goals. He would normally get a couple of goals or an assist in a game, but he never got six goals in a game. But he promised her he would do his best.

He put so much pressure on himself for that game. He was playing a team they had beaten before. I figured they would win. I kept thinking, *If he wins, tomorrow he'll have to play in the Final Four game at nine in the morning and then the championship game at one.* I was secretly hoping they would lose.

I felt selfish because I didn't want to be away from Kilee for that long. And then I thought, *That's awful. Why am I feeling this way? It's not right. I should be there supporting him.*

They lost that day, 1-0.

When you go through something like this, you know where you're supposed to be. You know what's important. A soccer game that day was not important, but watching Cameron play was. I was, again, torn.

Keeping a Piece of the Past

Something I really wanted that was in the house was the engagement ring Jason had given me. I wanted it for Kilee. Jason and I had always wanted to put the diamond into a pendant for her. We'd planned to do it when she turned sixteen, but we got her a car, so it was our intention to give it to her for Christmas. Jason and I are still friends, and we wanted Kilee to remember she came from two loving parents.

Just days after the explosion, we were at the house. I was crying, and Cameron was digging and digging because he knew how important it was to me to find that ring.

Our bedroom was so damaged that I never thought in a million years I would find the ring. I had lost a lot of jewelry in the fire, but those pieces didn't bother me. The only piece I wanted was that ring. Finding it was all that mattered to me.

We looked and looked and looked. I told Cameron, "It's OK, buddy, we don't need it. It's fine."

I went through the rest of the house to see what else was truly salvageable—not what the insurance company had deemed as salvageable.

But Cameron said, "No, Mom, I think I can find it."

We didn't have anything to dig with, so he grabbed a piece of wood that I think was a leg to a piece of furniture. I had already given up on the ring, but I told him we could look one last time before we left. Cameron started digging and digging. I saw the box, which was nearly destroyed. Cameron grabbed it and handed it to me. The ring was there. We didn't find any other jewelry, but Kilee's ring somehow had made it.

Cameron's room, though, was a complete loss. There was not even one piece of clothing saved from his room. I felt guilty about that. I gave him my credit card and told him to buy whatever he wanted. I can't tell you how much money he spent. And I didn't care because I wanted to do something nice for him. He had lost everything. That's part of the guilt I feel.

In trying to supplement for Cameron's loss, I go overboard. And honestly, it doesn't make it any better; but when you're going through it at the time, doing something feels better than doing nothing.

Recently, Cameron bought something online with my credit card, and I asked him how he did that without my card. He said he'd memorized the numbers. I should have known that his memory wouldn't let him down.

∾∾

Cameron:

The candy in my room that I was going to eat that night after basketball was gone.

It was heartbreaking to know all my Duke University stuff, stuff actually signed in person by team members, was gone. Several pairs of shoes, my Xbox, everything was gone.

It just stunk.

The only thing in my room that didn't get burned was my baby box. It had all of my baby pictures and awards and papers that Mom was proud of me for; she had added my cross-country certificate three weeks earlier. I found the box in the very corner of my room, in the space between the wall and my bed, out of the way.

Two days later, Mom and I went inside the house together. All the drywall was piled up over the top of it. Mom was bawling her eyes out, wanting to find the baby box. I made her go outside, and I went back into my room. I grabbed a pair of my socks that were ruined and put them on as gloves because I'm allergic to drywall, and started digging.

All of the sudden, I felt something hard. I kept digging. It was the hardwood floor that hadn't burned. I reached back farther, with the drywall on top of my arm, and hit a little metal handle. I threw all the drywall on top of my bed, which was only burnt in a few places, and I kept digging. I pulled it out, and the only part of my baby box that the fire had touched was the outer box. The top of it was black. But the rest of the box was perfectly blue, like normal.

Nothing inside was touched by the fire. It was perfect.

Growing Up a Little Brother

Lori:

Kilee played well with others; that is, until my nephew, Luke, was born. She was jealous and used to torment him. She was also super-jealous when I got pregnant with Cameron. She was two, so she was going through those tantrums.

My due date for Cameron was May 29, and I was freaking out because I didn't want my kids to have the same birthday. Kilee's was June 2. I wanted them to be able to enjoy their days separately. I made it past her third birthday party and was relieved. But Kilee had gotten so excited about having a baby sibling that she was willing to share her birthday.

Cameron was ten days overdue. They wanted me to try a natural birth with him because of complications I'd had with Kilee, but I never progressed after my water broke. I didn't feel the contractions, and they ended up having to do another emergency C-section on me.

Kilee was wearing her "Big Sister" T-shirt the day Cameron was born. All she wanted to do was hold him. She thought it was cool to be able to sit and hold him nonstop.

That continued as Cameron grew older. When he was about six months old, old enough to hold his own head up, Kilee would tow him around like one of her baby dolls. She loved babies and Barbie dolls, so she would put him into a stroller and push him around the house.

As they got older, they picked on each other a lot, with Kilee being the main culprit. She came across as nasty, and it just ate Cameron alive. He wanted her to like him and give him attention. He would do goofy things and act out to get her to notice him, and it just irritated her. (Now, he does those things to lighten her mood, and it makes her laugh.)

Teenagers go through these phases when they are maturing and their three-years-younger brother becomes an annoyance. I know this because I went through it with my brother, and Amy went through it with me, her younger sister. It's just something that happens. Cameron wanted Kilee's approval so badly. And because he has such a huge heart, it broke my heart to watch her not give him the time of day. I would tell her, "Come on, Kilee, just be nice to him." It got to the point where she would get into trouble because she would be disrespectful toward him.

They've grown so much closer since the accident, but they've also grown up. I think they've matured and realized how lucky they are to have each other. I think the accident has helped their relationship tremendously.

❧

Cameron:

My first memory of Kilee is her pushing me in a stroller. I don't even know how old I was, but I can remember her pushing me, me laughing the whole time, and she was happy. We were best buds until I was about five years old.

I was still little and wanted to play with little-kid toys, and she was eight and wanted to do what eight-year-old girls like to do. I don't really know what they like to do, but I was still sitting there wanting to play with dinosaurs. She started to hang out with her friends more. And of course I couldn't hang out with them because I was a boy.

When I was thirteen and Kilee was sixteen, we drifted apart even more at the beginning of that school year. I don't really know why, but she became more independent, I guess. She was always rude to me. But I knew she cared about me.

Kilee:

I always loved baby dolls, and my mom and dad bought me baby doll accessories like clothes and a stroller. When Cameron was little, I would put him in my baby doll stroller and push him around the house. I thought it was cool because he was like my own little baby doll. He never really cared. He enjoyed it, I thought. He's always been a kind of go-with-the-flow kind of person. He didn't worry about anything.

Now he's overbearing about everything.

We had a normal brother-sister relationship; we weren't best friends, but we didn't want to punch each other all the time—until I was about thirteen years old. Cameron was ten, and he was always annoying to me. I would tell Mom, "I can't stand him being around." I guess it was because he looked up to me being an older sibling. But he was just annoying about everything. Everything.

We went home from school every day at four o'clock. Cameron was obsessed with WWE. I knew it was fake, and he loved watching them punch each other, beat each other.

It was annoying.

We had TVs in our rooms, so I don't know why he would watch it in the living room. He insisted on getting the remote control every day and turning on WWE. I didn't want to watch it. Since we fought constantly about it, Mom made the rule that every other day I got the TV. Cameron never followed that rule. Every day, he'd run into the room, grab the remote, and hold on to it. Even if he was getting up to get something to eat in the kitchen, he'd still hold on to the remote. So one time, I followed him into the kitchen.

I started off asking him nicely, like, "Please, would you just give me the remote?"

Then I tried to take it from him.

He said, "No, you don't get the remote! I'm watching WWE."

I was about to punch him, and then I stepped back and took a breath. I thought, *OK, I'm not going to punch him.*

Instead, I looked around the kitchen and thought I'd scare him. I grabbed a knife. It wasn't a huge, long knife.

It was just a regular knife. I held it and said, "Give me the remote."

He ran out the door and stayed outside until Mom got home. I got the remote. I also got into trouble.

Before the accident, we bickered a lot. We never really talked to each other just because we wanted to. We had our differences, and we were really good at pointing them out to each other.

All that said, growing up with a sibling that close to my age was cool because we could do things together. When we were little, we had a lot of similar interests and would play together. It was fun until he got old enough to be a brat.

For a while before the accident, we were not close at all. He was always on my nerves. If I had a friend over, he would get on their nerves too. Just a bratty little brother. I never went out of my way to talk to him.

But I was protective over him sometimes.

Cameron was going through a chubby stage, and the kids at Ripley—it was when we both went to the same school—were mean to him. Even his so-called friends would call him fat and tell him he couldn't run. It would get on my nerves; and most kids in the fifth or sixth grade go through a chubby stage. Those who didn't go through that stage made fun of him for it. I made him sit with me on the bus. I never said anything to the kids making fun of him because I told him to ignore them and not even pay attention to them.

That November, before everything happened, Cameron was just a normal junior-high kid. He never thought about anything other than school. He never cared about where I was or asked Mom where I was or who I was with. Now, every time I'm not with him, he asks my Mom where I am, what I'm doing, who I'm with; he has to know everything. He always wants to know where everyone is, not just me, and I don't know why. He never used to care.

Another change since the accident is that we're close now.

We talk and hang out together. I take him with my friends to hang out, go out to eat. It's a better relationship. Maybe it's just both of us realizing that we both have each other. For however many years, we both have each other always.

When I was younger, people used to say I'd regret being mean to him or not having a good relationship with him. But I don't regret our past. I think we needed to have that relationship then, so we could get to the place where we are now.

Lori:

Cameron's life is forever changed.

His guilt comes from being at basketball practice, playing a sport, doing what he loves to do, instead of being at home protecting his sister. The first time he said anything to me, I thought I was going to be physically sick. I started crying immediately.

I didn't know to what extent he felt guilty, until the day he said to me, crying, "I should have been there."

"If you had been there, you might not be with us today or you could be in the same shape as Kilee," I said. "And then we would've been taking care of two people. Not only that, but your friend would have been with you. It's not for you to protect her. Don't feel guilty for not being there, because what would you have done?"

"I don't know..."

"You're brave for even telling me that you feel that way. Feeling guilty shows how sweet and caring you are, but you should never feel that way. Ever. You shouldn't have that weight on your shoulders."

Cameron is a worrier. He stresses over the smallest things. When he has his mind set about something, that's it. I tell him, "Whatever is going to happen is going to happen. Don't worry. You be the best person you can be, and everything will fall into place."

Because Cameron is super-smart and super-athletic, the attention was always on him and his achievements. I don't know why that was—for me, I always treated them equally.

Kilee's beautiful. She's always been beautiful. She's always been a pretty good athlete. She's always been pretty smart. But somehow Cameron always seemed to be the center of attention.

The attention shifted after the accident. All the attention was turned toward Kilee.

Cameron became really jealous of all the attention she was getting and that she still gets.

He has felt left out because I had to get Kilee ready for bed every night, and it took three hours in the beginning. I was the one who always took care of Cameron, but then,

I just couldn't. I didn't have the time. Wade took care of Cameron, taking him to school in the morning. That was hard on me because I was always in control of that and taking care of him. And I know it hurt Cameron's feelings.

I would explain to him that I had to get his sister ready for school.

"I know you do, Mom. It's OK."

He's broken down to me three times during this whole ordeal. During one of those times he said to me, "I do not want to be selfish. Look at all Sis has gone through. I don't want to say anything because I don't want people to think that I'm being selfish. But Mom, I don't know what to do with these feelings. I'm still having these feelings."

I told him, "It's OK. You're experiencing something normal that comes from a tragic situation. You're fine; you just have to express them. Don't hold them in."

I was proud of him for being selfless, but I was also concerned. Bottling that kind of thing up is when stuff can start happening to people. That's when they can go downhill.

I did notice a change in him—especially during basketball season—after Kilee came home. He was always full-blown, all-out when he played sports before. But during that basketball season, he had a hard time concentrating on the game. Kilee was always on his mind. The biggest thing he had on his mind was knowing where she was at all times.

"Where is she?"

"Is she safe?"

"Is she going to be OK today?"

"Is she driving somewhere?"

"Who's she with?"

"Are her hands going to be OK today?"

He's very protective and constantly concerned for her.

We had to watch what we said in front of him. Otherwise, he would get all sucked up into her not getting better; the worry would affect his daily life. When we'd leave the doctor, we'd tell Cameron all the good stuff and the progress, instead of the negative, so he didn't have to process that.

I think him watching Kilee has helped him realize you can go through anything in life and you can make it. I think he'll look back on this when he's an adult and be amazed by how well he did, how well the family did, and how well we all did together.

Cameron:

I stressed out about a lot more. With even the simplest things, like one homework problem, I would stress out.

It was hard to concentrate in school. That whole second quarter, I couldn't focus at all. There was no way to sit there and not think about everything else going on. I got two A's and five B's the second quarter. That's when it was the worst because I couldn't stop thinking about Kilee. *What happens if she touches this? What if she bumps into that?* I don't know how or why that changed in me. But since Kilee's made a full recovery, she's perfect, and I don't feel like I stress as badly anymore.

❧ ❧

Kilee:

I started calling Cameron my "big little brother" because he's bigger than me but also because he acts like an older brother. He's now very protective of me.

The first time I really noticed something different about Cameron was when I started to do stories in the media. He didn't want to say anything, but I could tell he was kind of feeling left out. He didn't want to intrude or get in the middle of anything I was doing. He just felt like staying back was the best thing. Even when he was interviewed, he didn't say much. He'd always be as brief as possible. He wouldn't tell anyone how he felt. He kept everything hidden. I think it's because he feels like he could've saved me if he'd been at the house. Mom told me Cameron thinks he could have helped, that he could have done something because he was supposed to have been home, too. But I want him to realize that is not how it is. There's nothing he could have done. But he has it locked in his head that he could have.

I don't want him to feel like that at all. I want everyone around me to know there is nothing anyone could have done. He couldn't have protected me, even if he had been at the house. But now he feels like he has to protect me in everything I do. I don't know how to make Cameron feel normal again—show him he doesn't have to worry about me or protect me. Everything is fine now.

Standing Up for Sis

Cameron:

I act like a big brother, physically and mentally.

When she went back to school, I worried about how people would act. I didn't want anyone to make her feel bad, saying anything to her about what happened. You just don't know. Maybe some random person would say things without thinking about it. I was worried about that happening.

Someone did say something at my school. During fifth period, a guy and a girl were talking about how Sis just wanted to get attention. That made me really mad. I went up to them and told the guy to keep his mouth shut. They didn't say anything else.

I didn't tell Sis about it because I didn't want her to believe what they said. I didn't want her to start thinking that.

ϟϟ

Kilee:

A few weeks into my stay at Shriners, my first memory of Cameron was on a Friday night when he had a basketball game. After his game, they brought him back because he stayed with us at Shriners on the weekends. He walked into my room and I could tell he wanted to hug me, so I stood up and he hugged me. Typically, we never hugged, ever. I asked him how his day was and how his week had gone, how his game went, like a normal older sibling would do. It was then that I realized something was different between us.

If I could tell him how I feel, I would say:

Cameron,

I know our relationship hasn't always been the greatest. I know we've had our fights, literally, and I know that most of the time we don't see eye to eye. But you are my baby brother, and I love you. We are all each other has for the rest of our lives. That's why I want you to know these things. I want you to know that none of this is your fault; it's no one's fault. It was a freak accident that happened, and nobody could have done anything about it, not even you. You would have been in the same situation as me, possibly even worse.

You blame yourself sometimes, and I want you to know you don't have to do that. I don't want you to do that. I don't want to see you beating yourself up over this, especially when you have no reason to. I want you to know I am OK; I am more than OK. I have handled this very well, and I couldn't have done that without you and the rest of our family. I want you to know I am so happy that our relationship has gotten so much better because of this.

We talk like brother and sister now, instead of arguing all the time. I love that our relationship has made it this far, and I can only hope it will get even better. I love having a normal relationship with you. You are very smart and talented, and I can't wait to see you grow and live your life. I am so happy with the young man you have become and are still becoming.

Love you, big little brother!

My Real Sis

Cameron:

I'm not a good singer. After everything, we'd be in the car and I would sing the high notes at the top of my lungs just to make Kilee laugh. She would laugh and laugh and not be able to stop. Just knowing that she could still laugh was a relief.

I see a story, a journey. Her scars are what she went through. I'd rather her have those scars than for her to not be here at all. If you really think about it, she shouldn't be here right now. Her purpose is to influence others and show everyone that even when life is the hardest, always have hope and it will work out perfectly in the end, just like her journey is.

Her story is positive and shows that a lot of bad can happen, but if you do what it takes to overcome it, it'll be OK in the end. My story is to always be there for someone no matter what, because you don't know what could happen. Time means everything, and everything happens in a split second.

I want to make sure Kilee is OK all of the time, wherever she is. I just want her to know that if something ever happens, I'll be there. I wasn't there for her that day, but I will be every day from now on.

The most important thing to me is that she is alive and everything is getting back to normal—just our everyday life and not stressing about the house or Sis healing; everything is fine. Back to the way it was…normal.

I thought she'd be worried about her scars, but somehow she's not. That amazes me. I'd probably be the biggest baby in the world. I don't know how, but she has been really, really strong during everything. Her mindset was that if she didn't do what she needed to, it would take longer to become fully recovered.

I've learned to be more caring now. I mess around a lot, but when someone I love leaves, I tell them I love them, because that morning I didn't tell Kilee that. She has taught me to never give up and always have hope.

These days, she's a lot more caring about me and now she's even protective over me. I knew she always felt that way about me, but she didn't know how to express it before. I feel like she does now. She'll say "I love you" before she leaves, and I'll tell her to be careful.

It's just different.

When I get home from doing something and she's there, she seems happy to see me, like maybe she was worried about me being out.

I do wish I could have been there to help her, but I know that I probably wouldn't be standing here if I had been standing there.

CHAPTER NINE

Changes and Milestones

Kilee:

Before my accident, I had a boyfriend, someone I'd known for many years because our parents were close friends. We'd been together for quite a while, and on the day of the explosion, he was one of the first people at the hospital. He stayed with me while I was at Shriners, and when I came home, he still supported me.

I felt loved, but I knew something had changed. I guess part of me was grateful that he was standing by me. I'm sure a lot of guys would not want to be with a girl who needed so much care, therapy, and help getting back to normal.

But our relationship had never been perfect. (I know no one's really is.) And after the accident, things just never felt right again. I was young, but I could see that I wasn't happy anymore, and that our relationship wasn't good for me. Maybe not for him, either. He already had graduated from high school, and we both just needed to move on.

We broke up not long after I was on *The Doctors*. My boyfriend had acted very jealous after I'd met Justin Bieber, and that was the breaking point.

It was kind of hard to think about my life without him, but at the same time, I was feeling better and getting stronger every day. It was time for me to really have a fresh start and to figure out who I was, on my own. It was the right thing to do.

Junior Prom

When my junior prom came in the spring, I was torn about the whole thing. My focus was on my healing and finding a dress that I was comfortable wearing, especially since homecoming had been a complete bust.

I thought, *I didn't even have a good time at homecoming. Do I want to go to prom?* But then my friend asked me, and I did want to go because I didn't want to miss out on my junior prom. It was actually a lot of fun, more than I expected. We didn't exactly dance the night away; I kind of sat there and watched everyone—which I think is better anyway.

I had gone to the doctor a couple of weeks before prom and they told me I didn't have to wear any of my garments that day. I was looking for a long-sleeved dress, though, because my arms were still sensitive. I wanted a short-sleeved dress, but my mom was worried that if I bumped someone or someone bumped me, who knows what could've happened. She was scared to let my arms out.

I had been looking for a dress that would cover up everything. While Amy was at the mall, she saw a dress.

It was my size. It covered my arms. It covered my back. It covered my legs. It was my style: glittery, blingy, pretty. It was perfect. It was me. It's a dress I would've picked out before the accident.

It was long-sleeved, bluish-purple with jewels and mermaid style. It was sparkly at the top. It was much more my style than my homecoming dress had been. And it would be the first time I would be out of my garments.

Lori:

A few days before prom, Kilee cried because the splotchy, red blemishes on her back showed through her prom dress and she wanted to go without her garments. She realized we could fix it and was OK with it.

It broke my heart.

The continuous strength she has is remarkable. I've been told that her attitude is a lot like mine. But I've learned that her strength is beyond anything I could ever do. And I don't think she sees it. She's blinded by it. I think she knows she's strong, but I don't think she realizes how strong she really is.

I was worried about how she would feel, not how I felt, but how she would feel about getting those garments off her arms and having her hands exposed that day. I was worried for her, and then that day, I thought, *Wow, she's going to be fine. She doesn't even care.*

Her scars are not who she is—she's the same Kilee, but with a life redefined.

Just to see her on prom day…she was beautiful. Just stunning.

Her dress was beautiful. You could see a little bit of scarring on her hands, but I wouldn't have thought anything about it until people said, "Wow, her hands look really good."

I was thinking, *That's what you're seeing because you're not there every day. We've gone through this since the beginning. You think that looks good? Yeah, you should have seen her before.*

That's what it feels like. Like, you have no idea. For me, it's completely different as her mother. For me, it's not a sight of pity, how good she looks. I look at her as Kilee. I don't see her scars anymore. And when I do have a moment when I think about how different she looks, I remember, she's alive. She's here. And that's what's gotten me through this. Her life could've been taken that day, and we're very fortunate it wasn't.

ഗ്രൂ

Kilee:

On the day of prom, May 9, I woke up early for my hair and makeup. I was really nervous because there were producers from another TV show coming to do a story on prom and the whole day.

In February, they had contacted Mom and told her they were a German-based company and had offices out of New York. It was after I did *The Doctors*, so I felt like I was ready to do it.

They wanted to shoot a big event, but Mom told them there wasn't really anything going on until prom in May. I figured they wouldn't come two months later. But they did.

But unlike the way I felt in January doing a TV show, I was starting to feel more like myself. Normal. I was back in school, and I was going to prom. I felt like things were starting to settle down a bit, and I didn't really want to do another show.

They made me set up my room and make my bed. My room was eighty degrees because of the huge lights they'd set up. They wanted a backstory, so they interviewed me for four hours at the house—with my mom, then separately, and then together. Then they wanted to shoot me putting lotion on, but I don't normally do that—my mom does. So they had her put lotion on my hand.

Later that day, we met them at the salon. They were telling me what to do and how to do it.

I was thinking, *This is not your day. This is prom. I have to be at certain places at certain times, and you need to follow me there. I'm not going by your schedule.*

There were two people following me. It was hard to understand the guy who had a gigantic camera.

While the reporter was asking me about my life story, the videographer was setting up the huge camera. The hair salon was tiny, with one lady doing hair, and there was a line of people behind me waiting to get their hair done for prom. The TV crew was taking up the entire salon.

It was weird to have girls there that I knew from my school talking to me in between me answering questions to the reporter. And they were hearing everything I was saying. It was awkward.

Finally it was my turn to get my hair done. With it being really short, I figured it wouldn't take that long. The reporter put the microphone on me. She put one on my hairdresser. They set up the camera right next to us, looking through the mirror at me. As she was doing my hair, they were asking me questions.

I didn't think this was what was going to happen. I didn't think they would be there for the entire day. They even made me answer questions with my eyes closed so they could see me getting my eye shadow applied.

They literally didn't leave my side until I went home to change into my dress. I didn't want them to follow me there, so we told them to meet us at Front Street on the Ohio River where we'd take photos.

Lori:

Prom was the first time Kilee felt free. She was out for the night, out of the house, and out of her garments for the first time.

It was also the first time she was away from me for an entire evening. I told myself I wouldn't constantly text her while she was out because I wanted her to have a good time and be a normal sixteen-year-old girl.

My friend, who also had a daughter in Kilee's prom group, asked me if I wanted to catch up with the group in downtown Cincinnati to photograph them eating, etc. I said no, because I wanted her to have that privacy, freedom, and the ability to enjoy herself with her friends. It was the first time she was able to really go and do anything on her own. Like, really on her own. And she had a great time.

She even slow danced, and she's not a big dancer. It was like her friends brought her back to life again. She was comfortable around them all. Without her garments, everyone saw her hands for the first time, and they were loving and supportive. They were glad she was there.

After prom, Kilee realized it was time for her to move on with her life and past her previous relationship.

Life is going to happen the way it's meant to happen. There's nothing you can change about that. It's about how Kilee approaches everything thereafter, and that includes dating.

CHAPTER TEN

Back to Normal?

Kilee:

Throughout that first summer of wearing garments in 2015, there were times when I felt uncomfortable and times when I felt comfortable. I was constantly having to adjust to new things and new feelings, but while I was adjusting, I was able to spend a lot of time with my family. We went on multiple trips, and as the summer went on, I got more and more comfortable. Today, I look back and feel nothing like I did that summer, but in those summer moments, I felt like a completely new person compared to who I'd been before.

That summer, our whole family went to Key Largo. On that trip, we did things like swimming with dolphins, which I decided to sit out because I wasn't feeling so comfortable. My mom and I also met my DECA team in Orlando. The team had made it to nationals because of how well it had done on a project about the fundraiser it conducted for me and Shriners. On that trip, I tried getting back to wearing more normal clothing and had some challenges. Later, we went to Norris Lake in Tennessee with a bunch of family friends, and I got into the water for the first time since the summer of 2014.

That summer was one I will never forget, because it was the first time for a while that I felt like my old self. I felt like I was seeing the end of my recovery road. For so long, the recovery process seemed never-ending, and this was the first time I felt I was getting somewhere with it. These trips were necessary for me to see that I was making good progress and that everything I was working for was becoming worth it in the end.

Lori:

We are living in today, and every day is like a vacation to us. We are excited for each day as if it were a vacation day.

As Kilee's mother, it was hard to watch her not be able to wear a bathing suit on vacation or shorts when the temperatures were in the upper eighties. I knew she was hot.

I tried to stay positive and remind her it was temporary.

Her personality hasn't changed at all through all of this. People who aren't with her every day cannot fathom that she is truly this strong, truly happy, after what she's been through. They can't understand how she's able to overcome this. That's not to say that she won't have bad days, because she will, and she has. People think your appearance defines you, and it doesn't. It's who you are inside and how you treat people.

Kilee:

Before, I was a normal teenage girl. I did things with my friends, went to school, and that's about it. I never had to worry about anything.

After the accident, I had much more to worry about. My parents' time, school, my future, my recovery and healing, everything. I couldn't go home and do whatever I wanted, and it made things a lot harder than they should have been, on me and on my family.

It's made me who I am today, though. The real struggle was becoming the person I used to be. I loved being that person and I wanted her back. I went through a time that I changed a little, but I realized that wasn't who I wanted to be.

My normal did change for a little bit because of how used to everything I was, like my parents helping me bathe and go to the bathroom. I was so used to having them do everything for me that it became normal, and it took a little bit for me to realize it wasn't. I could start to do things on my own. After I realized that, I started to be my old self and was able to get back to my "normal."

Routine Brings Normality

Lori:

The family got into a routine throughout the changes and getting back to a new normal.

Per our shared custody, Kilee was with me eight days, Jason six days. But I saw her every day. I was taking her to Shriners. I was taking her to school every day. I did her stretching with her, unless she stayed with Jason, and he did it first thing in the morning. I would stretch Kilee at night before she went to Jason's, just to help as much as possible because Jason had gone back to work and I still wasn't back full-time. Plus, I had Wade to help me.

When you stretch her first thing in the morning, then take her to school in the morning, pick her up at one, go to Shriners, come home, do an hour-long stretching at five o'clock and then again at eight o'clock, followed by a bath and a lotion massage before bed, it takes a toll on you. You get exhausted. We did that routine for four months straight.

At the three-month mark, we were washing her back, which was sensitive and still really pink. Kilee perspired a lot, especially during therapy sessions, so her back took longer to heal.

In March, she dropped down to two days a week at Shriners and one day at orthopedic therapy (which helped her with her mobility and endurance). That was when she got better and better and better. It helped her with her soccer. She couldn't even throw the ball before that. Once she was better with her endurance, she was transferred to a sports therapist, which she continued with for three times a week for two months.

In May, Shriners was impressed with how well Kilee was doing. They told us to slowly transition her out of her gloves.

I realized, *Wow, she's really going to be OK.*

People don't realize how much hard work it was. They just see Kilee's beautiful smile.

On June 1, Shriners took Kilee out of her gloves. She couldn't even go to the bathroom by herself until then. She was also out of her garments and wore Spanx instead of the vest. The vest was really tight and made her arms tingly. Plus, the vest didn't fit right anymore because Kilee had gained back some of her weight.

She had worn the vest and garments around her waist for so long that it had pushed around her stomach skin, reshaping her abdomen. There were indentations from the garments, and they bothered her.

Kilee was glad to have the garments gone.

Even though she wore Spanx shorts and a Spanx top, she was cautious about everything. She was scared that if she did something wrong, it was going to impact her in a bad way. She still wore her garments at night, too paranoid to go without them. She also still had to be massaged with lotion on tight spots—massaging, massaging, massaging. Her nurses told us they would eventually loosen up and go away. Kilee's right arm was the worst.

Dad's Wedding

Kilee:

The explosion put a hold on my dad and Brooke's wedding because they wanted me to be comfortable with it and they wanted me to be in the wedding. Once I was home from Shriners, Dad asked me if I was OK with him asking Brooke to marry him.

We helped him.

Brooke's sister, Cameron, and I went to the house and set up lights and rose petals. We were in the bathroom hiding, and Brooke was shocked. She had no idea who did it. We had put a heart on the bed made out of lights that looked like candles.

Dad asked her and she said yes.

They got married a few months later, in May.

It was an outdoor wedding at Ault Park in Cincinnati. Cameron, Brooke's sister, and I were in the wedding. There weren't a lot of people there at all, maybe twenty, and it was about ten minutes long. Then it was over. It was really pretty.

They wanted to make sure I was OK with it because I had to wear my garments still, and my sleeves and gloves. They weren't sure I would be comfortable in a dress.

When we went dress shopping, it was hard because we couldn't find anything that would work with my garments. I had to wear a long-sleeved shirt under my dress because I didn't want anything to hurt or scratch up my back and arms. My dress was a tannish-cream color, long and long-sleeved.

A First for Everything

A normal vacation for me is going to the beach with my family, laying out all day, and going to a nice dinner at night. That is how most of our vacations used to go. My normal vacations now are going to the same places and doing the same things. Nothing has really changed, and that is really important to me because my family and I always look forward to our vacations every year.

When I went to Key Largo in April, it was the first time I'd gone there.

I knew it was going to be hot—at the time, I was still wearing my sleeves, leggings, and all of my garments. I just wore T-shirts with my garment sleeves underneath. It was a little weird, especially when I saw people looking, but I didn't care.

This trip was the first time I wore a headband in my hair. My hair was starting to get longer, and I didn't know what to do with it. I had just bought headbands and thought I would try one. When I did, I was excited that it didn't look terrible and it got my hair out of my face. I ended up wearing them every day after that.

When we vacationed before, I was really excited to have fun with all of our family who went. I was ready to get out of town for a little while.

Now, I know it doesn't matter where I am. It matters who I'm with and if I have a good time—whether it's in Florida or Georgetown. I was just glad to be with my family having fun.

Lori:

When we left Key Largo, we went to Orlando to meet Kilee's DECA team, and Kilee was happy.

The team made it to the final round. I hadn't seen Kilee that excited since she met Justin Bieber! It was her story, and they won for her story. Before the accident, Kilee would have been working on this project. This year, it was about her. It was special for her.

In their category, they placed in the top twenty out of two hundred teams from all over the world.

But being around that many people was different.

In the back of my mind, I was cautious and wondering if I was going to have to talk to Kilee, comfort her, encourage her, and reassure her that this is all temporary and that we're going to get through this. Or, would she get through it and be OK?

People stared because of her gloves. They looked like Isotoner gloves, and it was hot and humid in Florida. It didn't bother Kilee, and as long as it didn't bother Kilee, I didn't care.

Her hair had started to grow back, and it was the first time she had worn a headband.

She broke out on her back from the heat and the sweat from her garments, so she started to wear Spanx.

She tried a regular bra. By the end of the night, she came to me and said, "You've got to get this off me. It's cutting into my back. I don't feel right. It's not comfortable. You've gotta get my garments back on me."

We put them back on, and she felt better.

Normally on vacation Kilee would wear a cute little bikini. And in more recent months, that's exactly what she's done. She's brave like that. It's awesome that she feels that comfortable in her own skin, scars and all.

Lake Cumberland, Amy's Wedding

In August, Kilee went to Lake Cumberland a day early with Amy to help her with her wedding. Kilee wore a sweatshirt because it was around sixty-five degrees and cloudy—very uncommon for August at Lake Cumberland in Kentucky. Sometimes I think the weather was a sign for Kilee to be comfortable. She fit in wearing long sleeves, unlike wearing gloves in ninety-degree Florida. Plus, she didn't have to worry about getting burned that day.

The next day, when we all got there, we spent the day on the boat. Kilee put a beach towel over her legs and was comfortable.

Kilee:

Lake Cumberland was probably my favorite trip of the year.

I went a day earlier than my family with my Aunt Amy, her soon-to-be husband, Nick, and Loren. Loren begged me to go early with them, and I finally gave in and said I would. I warned them they would have to put the lotion on me and put my garments on me at night, and they didn't care. It was the first time I was away from home without my mom or dad to help me with lotion and my garments at night. It was also the first time I felt I could trust anyone else to help with my garments.

Everyone's families were there, and that was the first time that had ever happened. So that was a very special trip for everyone. It was the first trip I felt totally comfortable. I was able to be free of my garments during the day, and I could wear anything I wanted. The doctor even approved it, which made me feel a lot better about it. I wore whatever I wanted and didn't care what people thought. I wore skirts and dresses, and I even had someone fix my hair. It was the first time I felt OK about my hair and outfits in a very, very long time.

I was finally starting to feel more like myself.

I live my life and do some things differently than before the accident in some aspects, but I have gotten used to that. I am perfectly fine that some things are different.

Living Life Like a Vacation Every Day

Lori:

With vacations, you're excited and you have that feeling like you can't wait to get there and be on vacation. We don't feel that way anymore. We're excited to go, but it's not about getting away.

We travel a lot. We always have, ever since the kids were little. Some years we do five or six vacations. We always looked at them as spending time together. But now, we spend so much time together every day that the vacations are just a change in scenery with the people we love. We spend time together every chance we get, not just on trips out of town.

The perspective has totally changed.

When something like this tragedy happens, you are truly grateful for every moment, every second you get with the people you love, no matter what you're doing or where—the movies, going out to eat, vacations. You're that much more excited to do the little things with the people who matter the most, every day, not just a few weeks a year.

We don't wait anymore to live our lives. And we don't wait for vacation to count every blessing.

Our tragedy has made us realize what life is about. This is life, and you can't change it. When a tragic situation happens, there is nothing you can do to change the past. But you can change things going forward.

Every day, there's so much to look forward to. I look at Kilee and I know we can make it through anything.

CHAPTER ELEVEN

Kilee Gives Back

Kilee:

Everyone wanted to help while I was at Shriners. And they did. All in their own way.

A little girl gave me her baby doll. It was an adorable redheaded doll. Her mom told my parents that it was her favorite doll, and for some reason the little girl wanted to give it to me; she said she thought I needed the doll more than she did. It was the sweetest thing ever, especially coming from a six-year-old little girl. The little girl had never even met me.

The doll sat on my counter in my room while I was at Shriners, next to a bunch of things that people had given me. I was asking my mom where each thing had come from. I remember going down the line, and then I asked about the doll. It melted my heart and made me happy.

There were so many people doing so many things, even just sending cards that said, "I hope you get better!"

Fundraising

It felt really good that my DECA club, kids at school, and friends, family, and strangers in the community were raising awareness and money for me while I was at Shriners. It wasn't just my friends. It was the whole school, even people whom I had never talked to. It meant a lot to me that they cared so much. It was cool that that many people wanted to help in any way they could. And it spread throughout both communities, Ripley and Georgetown: the town where I went to school and the town where I live.

It was cool to know they all wanted to help. It made me realize I, too, needed to do something to help people once I was able.

Lori:

There was such an outpouring of support with not only money, but in prayers and well wishes too. People came up to me all the time to tell me how amazing Kilee is. The community has supported her like she is their very own, in any way they can.

We're grateful for everything. It almost makes you feel guilty that people are doing so much for you. I've always been the giver. If someone needed clothes or money, whatever the situation was, I would help however I could. I sometimes donate anonymously because I don't want people to know it's me. To have others reach out and help us has been quite a change.

The first fundraiser was Kisses for Kilee, through her school, the students, and the DECA program, while Kilee was still at Shriners. The DECA program, which Kilee was part of, took on the fundraising through the school as its annual project.

The team's efforts were especially appreciated because these kids were Kilee's best friends, and she would have been involved in such a project had the explosion not happened. They sold Hershey's Kisses at lunch and sold bracelets with "Pray for Kilee" and "Hugs for Kilee" written on them.

An anonymous donor donated the "Hugs for Kilee" bracelets, and a local bank paid for the "Pray for Kilee" bracelets. All of the money raised was donated into an account at the bank. But we had no control over who was doing what with the money and who was raising money with Kilee's name on it or where it was going.

"Baskets for Brookbank" raised money with two basketball games in December, one at Ripley and one at Georgetown—Kilee and Cameron's schools, respectively.

We didn't even tell anyone Kilee was home, let alone that she was going to the game. She got home on a Thursday and went to the Georgetown game on Saturday for the second "Baskets for Brookbank" game. She wanted to go, and she was persistent. She had just gotten off all of her medication, so we were shocked she wanted to go.

I asked her, "Are you sure you want to go? Are you OK with this?" I mean, she couldn't even walk without help, and we knew she'd have to go up steps and bleachers. Plus, she had on a toboggan because she had no hair. She couldn't move her hands, her fingers; everything was still stiff. She had open wounds everywhere still. She just wasn't in good health. But she was home, and she was determined to get there no matter what.

After we were there for a bit, I said to her, "Kilee, it's not that bad, is it?" but her friends were standoffish. They didn't know what to say to her, didn't know if they could touch her or hug her. It was uncomfortable watching it because it was as though they were scared of her. They were trying to make her comfortable by not saying too much to her.

She confided to me, "It's kind of weird," and I said, "I know, but it'll be OK. It's good that you're getting out and seeing people for the first time since everything happened."

She said, "Yeah, I know."

And less than five minutes later, they announced her in the stands. None of us knew that she was going to be announced at the game. Kilee broke down and cried. Of course, I was crying too. It was a nice gesture to announce her like that.

A former track coach who had coached Amy and me when we were in high school absolutely adored Amy. She was a great runner, winning first place often. He came up to me at that basketball game. He told me how well Kilee looked and that he'd been praying for her. He handed me two hundred dollars to give to her that day. I thought, *No, you're retired. Don't give us money.* But he insisted. I gave the money to Kilee.

Months later, I was at Cameron's soccer game, and the coach was taking the money at the gate.

He came over to me and started talking to me while I was watching the game. The team was struggling; I was getting frustrated. He chatted with me for about twenty minutes or so, and then he said he had something to tell me. I looked at him. Usually he's joking or cutting up about Amy and some funny story about her in driver's ed. But he said to me, in all seriousness and looking straight ahead: "I pray for you and that girl every day. I've been pulling for her since this happened. She's a special girl."

That's been most people's reaction to her.

We don't want pity for Kilee; she's doing great. It's all about what you're willing to do to turn it around. And that's exactly what she's done. She said from the moment she got home, "I can sit and soak up all the sympathy and sorrow and keep being miserable, or I can do something about it."

I knew she had a good outlook on it, and she was going to do something about it.

Directing Good Deeds

Kilee:

To have the entire community want to give back to me felt amazing, but a little overwhelming too.

So many people sent cards, and I enjoyed getting them and reading them, but there were so many that I couldn't possibly thank everyone individually. Kids from different schools sent me a blanket they had made, cards they made, and so much more. It did make me very happy hearing from the little kids, because the cards they sent were funny. It gave me a laugh every once in a while—and I needed that.

It was a great feeling to know I had so many people supporting me. People I didn't even know sent me cards, gifts, or money. I knew they felt like they should help in some way, and some people thought that was the best way to help. The money wasn't needed but very appreciated. I felt loved from all over.

For me, giving back all started long before I was even out of the hospital. Really, it started before I knew what was happening. People felt the need to give. And give to me. But I wanted others to have the help they were giving. So I thought of the best way to do that. And that was giving back to Shriners and its families. I wanted to give as a way to thank everyone who gave their time, love, and support to me and on behalf of me.

About a week after I came home from Shriners, I realized just how much the staff had helped me and how much they help so many others. Once I was home, I had to do it all on my own. I appreciated them so much more. If they hadn't been there for me for those thirty-eight days getting me ready to be on my own, I don't know how I would have turned out.

I wanted—needed—to do something.

If there wasn't a Shriners hospital in Cincinnati, I don't think my outcome would have been this good. I was really lucky to have one close to me. There would have been some serious issues, and who knows where I'd be.

There are many other kids. Most people only think of themselves and their recovery, but I think of myself and I know I'm through that stage. Fortunately, I no longer need all of that care—but there are kids who do.

People sent money to me when I was in the hospital, and I realized there was so much money that I couldn't possibly need it all. After I came home from the hospital, my parents wanted to know what I planned to do with all the money. I wasn't sure what I should do, so I talked to my mom about everything, and she thought we should donate most of the money back to Shriners, since it is based off donations. I agreed with her, so we donated most of the money to them. I felt like it was the right thing to do.

Starting the nonprofit foundation Kilee Gives Back gave what I'm doing a name and shows that I'm always going to give back. So many wanted to donate money to me directly, but really, that's not what I wanted. I never wanted it for myself. I want it for Shriners. I think so many wanted to help but didn't know how, and that's why I want to give it to those who need it most.

In a way, with the foundation, I am directing all of that help into one place, where it can do the most good. I've seen firsthand how this money helps people. I want to continue to help other kids get better, like I was able to.

Lori:

Immediately after getting the donations, we thought we would give the money back. It started the second day we were at Shriners. All these people wanted to give us money and give us this and give us that. It was a very generous gesture.

Through Shriners, we put out a statement to the media that if anyone wanted to donate money, to donate to Shriners Cincinnati in Kilee's honor. We received about twenty-five papers from Shriners for donations they had received on Kilee's behalf. But it seemed like people really wanted to do more. I guess it's that urge to do something for someone in need and not knowing what to do. We didn't know a lot of the people donating; they were doing it out of the goodness of their hearts. Many who held fundraisers in Kilee's name knew we would donate that money to Shriners. At an expensive college, Kilee could have had her first year paid for, but that didn't feel right. This money needed to go to someone who needed treatment at Shriners.

But before that statement to the media, the donations to our family were out of control.

I got a phone call from a church that wanted to donate money, toothbrushes, blankets, toothpaste, and all the necessities to us. Someone had posted on Facebook that we needed all of those items, and I felt like, "No, no, no, no. Go donate that stuff to someone who truly needs it."

The nice gestures could sometimes be overwhelming. I wanted to say, "Give us time. Our house just burned to the ground. Our daughter is in the hospital; we don't even know if she's going to make it."

The Kilee Gives Back Foundation gives us control over where donated money goes and how it helps others. We want to help kids in Shriners burn units across the country—through paying bills, visiting with them, giving them care packages.

We've already accomplished one of our major goals: to raise $100,000 and have a family suite named in Kilee's honor. We've surpassed that number, and soon we'll be able to see her name on the wall at Shriners Cincinnati.

Paying It Forward

Kilee:

Four months after the explosion, I, along with DECA and my teacher, donated a check for almost $32,000 to Shriners, thanks to the fundraisers done while I was recovering.

Since everyone wanted to give, I wanted people to have a place to give that money, one central giving organization—that's what the Kilee Gives Back Foundation is. I wanted to continue the momentum of giving.

My stepdad, Wade, said, "Behind every door in this facility, miracles happen," and I want to make sure that keeps going. I know Shriners is a non-profit that relies on donations, and I wanted to help them like they helped me. It felt amazing to be able to give back to the thousands of kids who are treated every year at Shriners, regardless of their families' ability to pay.

Lori:

Kilee is quiet and polite and has a deep-seated motivation to not only recover, but also to inspire others to do the same, all while giving back to those who need it.

That night, after donating to Shriners, she was standing with me in the bathroom, dripping wet from having been in the shower. I was patching her open wounds, as I did every night, when she turned to me and said, "I really want to continue to give back."

"What do you mean?"

"I'd like to do something for Shriners. What can I do?"

I told her I'd get her information and we'd go from there.

After a shower the next night, we were talking about it again, and I told her with it being the end of February already, we were left with either a gala or a golf outing. I know how golf scrambles work because I do a few charity ones every year. She thought that might be good. At that point it was just talking—she had a lot going on, getting back into school, recovering, and regaining some normalcy in her life.

Foundation Goals

We were at the most vulnerable time in our lives, and we were fortunate enough to have a Shriners hospital in Cincinnati. The entire organization went out of their way to help us in every aspect you can imagine. There wasn't just one doctor involved. There was a team of twenty people involved in Kilee's care and her case. Nurses, counselors, doctors, nurse practitioners, therapists. From the get-go, she was well taken care of.

There is a feeling we got, a need to return a favor. No matter how many times we said thank you, it never seemed like enough. We felt like our story had a purpose, and our story could help people.

I see the foundation primarily helping patients in need and their families. It could help with medical bills for kids all over the country.

We want to visit with families who are at Shriners, scared and struggling. Kilee wants to be an advocate for Shriners. I didn't want her talking to people in hospitals until she was healed—physically and emotionally. I wanted her to be comfortable with herself.

But she was ready.

We want people to know they can get through this, and once they meet Kilee and see her spirit and her kindness, they're amazed. She's shy, but to help someone, she'll do anything. I could see it in Kilee's eyes when she was at Shriners. When she saw the other kids who were burned, it broke her heart. She was devastated for them. Kilee wants to tell them all, "It'll be OK. It takes time and healing.

And it doesn't matter if you have a scar. It doesn't define you."

We also want to give them a care package with Kilee's book inside so they can read our story and see there is light. There is hope. And there is life after tragedy.

Life is about giving back, helping others, and bettering yourself.

I served my purpose. I gave back, and I shared my story. I shared my nightmare. I shared my hardship to make something better for anyone else who is going through a similar situation. Something good can come out of something bad, and it normally does. You have to be willing to take on the battle, along with the ups and downs of it. You never want to forget what happened; it's a reminder to keep moving forward.

Celebrity Golf

We asked Justin Bieber's management team if they'd like to be involved, and they jumped at the chance to help Kilee. Thus, the golf outing became a celebrity event.

The best part of my day during that time was coming home and sitting around for hours talking with Cam, Kilee, and Wade about the event. It was something we created together as a family.

Everything Cam and Kilee have done has been neat. Watching how much they've grown and learned from all of this is remarkable. The fact Cam wants to give back in the same way Kilee does and the family does, at only sixteen years old, is incredible.

Kilee and Cameron worked on the golf fundraiser in 2015 together. It went smoothly and was a success, especially for the first year.

We had eighty golfers. With volunteers and everyone else, 125 people came out for the celebrity golf tournament.

We did well on our silent auction, which included $500 for a meet-and-greet with Justin Bieber; $3,500 for a custom-made Verdin bell that included Kilee's hands and the foundation logo; and $1,500 to throw out the first pitch at a Reds game. The last two were both donated to Shriners. A child from Shriners got to throw out a first pitch.

I didn't realize how many generous people there are in the world until we went through this tragedy.

Our friends and family have been amazing through all of this. Most of them were at the golf outing volunteering. I feel grateful, all of the time. And I don't want to keep telling them I'm grateful because it's like a broken record, but it's never enough. That day, they were texting me, thanking me for allowing them to be part of the day. It should be us thanking them again, but they're thanking us because they know how remarkable Kilee is. They've all been there from day one; they know how far she's come. They may not have seen her struggle with baths and everything else she had to deal with, but they've seen her everyday struggles like opening a door or a can of pop, or putting on mascara.

When I went up to the stage area to make the final announcement about the raffle prizes and split-the-pot, I looked out into the crowd and I couldn't believe how many people stayed after golf. I'd say 115 stayed; very few golfers had left.

I've been to a lot of golf scrambles, and there are never that many people who stay past dinner. At scrambles, even I would look at my watch and think about all I needed to do on a school night when I got home. To see this many people still there, still supporting Kilee and her foundation, was amazing. I was in awe.

But like I said, my favorite part of the day was sitting there with Kilee, Cameron, and Wade at the house afterward. I was on one side of the couch, Wade was on the other, Kilee was on the floor, and Cameron grabbed a dining room chair and sat in the middle of us all. It touched my heart to see how important the day was for them; they had put so much effort into it. I mean, they're teenagers, and I have to remember sometimes that they have a life they're trying to figure out; they're trying to figure out what they want to do and who they want to be. But in that moment, this was very special to them, and it's what they wanted to do. This was where they wanted to be. It meant more to me than I could ever explain.

I want the foundation to help Kilee and Cameron mentally and emotionally, to give them the gratification of helping others, because I feel you should pay it forward. There's such a reward when you know you're helping others. And you can't get through life on your own. It doesn't work that way.

In September 2016, we held our second annual golf scramble, and this one raised even more money for Shriners. We were able to present the hospital with a check for more than $55,000, in addition to a huge, custom-made clock from Verdin that is displayed at the facility.

In October, we partnered with Kendra Scott jewelry on a special, one-day promotion that raised almost $900 for Shriners, and we routinely receive donations through the Kilee Gives Back website.

We have a lot of goals set for the foundation, but it's a work in progress for us. It's overwhelming to feel this good about accomplishing something that helps so many.

Kilee:

I want the foundation to raise as much money as possible, just because I know how it is. I feel like it's my job to help them in some way. I want to bring awareness to Shriners also, so that everyone can know about it and feel the way I feel about it; then they'd want to give back too.

The golf event was more my mom's idea. She plays in one every year, and she thought it would be a good idea and a good money maker, since she knows how well the one she plays in does. The celebrity thing came about because she had connections with the Cincinnati Reds and JB, and she knew she could get more connections.

It was important to me, because if my mom thought that it would do well, then I believed her, and I really wanted to raise a lot of money for Shriners. I wanted to repay Shriners for all it has done for me and other people across the world.

I was surprised at how well the golf event went. You'd think the first time would have a few things go wrong, but luckily, nothing did.

It was a little weird to have all of these people come out for me. You don't think about it, and then when you realize it, it's like, well, if I weren't here, they wouldn't even be here at all. It made me happy that it meant that much to each of them to be there for me. It made me feel special, and I loved knowing that everyone participating in the tournament knew the money was going to Shriners. Not very many people know about Shriners, so it brought awareness to them as well.

What It's All About

Lori:

It's not all about the money. It's what that money is doing for the hospital, saving children's lives. Without the money, they wouldn't be able to do what they do and what they did for Kilee.

We also have donated a book to each patient who is admitted to the ICU at three Shriners burn centers. We thought that would be a way to give back long-term, showing our life and how we lived it in and out of Shriners. At the start of our journey, there wasn't anyone who would provide comforting information or share their story in a way that would help. We hope Kilee's story gives others some encouragement, some strength, and some idea of what to expect in their recovery.

Kilee's story is a remarkable one, and there are a lot of kids who don't make a recovery like she has. I want other Shriners parents to know they need to do as they're told. They need to help their child through those eight hours of total work that is done each day. If they do that, they're helping the child get better—if they stick with it, then the child will likely be OK. If they don't stick with it, then they're setting up for failure.

Our friend who has a daughter who was burned as a child told us, "Do what they tell you to do," but there wasn't anyone to explain to us what that meant. At the time, you cannot comprehend what that means.

Kilee has scarring all over her body, but it's not what you look at. She can do everything that she could before, she's beautiful, and wow, she has this great outlook on everything. That's what we want other people to know and see, instead of going into this life-changing event with no knowledge about what it's really like for the child and their family, especially once they leave the hospital.

Showing Off Every Scar

Kilee:

My story has a purpose.

I love to talk to other patients and show them they can

get to the other side of healing and that scars are beautiful. I know what it's like to have someone tell you it's going to be OK.

I had a former patient—a family friend's daughter— come talk to me while I was there, and it truly did help. She said that if I ever needed anyone to talk to, I could call her. My mom asked me if I wanted to talk to someone, and I told her it wouldn't hurt. My parents agreed with me. They asked her to come in, and she came when she could. The first time she came, I was nervous because I had never met her and I didn't know what she would say. I wanted to ask her questions about her recovery and about how she is now. It ended up going very well. She stayed and talked to my mom and me for an hour in my room. When we were finished talking, I felt much better about everything; I didn't realize it then, but now I know that I want to help someone like she helped me. She really did help me feel better about going home and getting back to my normal life. I want to give others hope too.

You never know when something is going to change in your life, and this changed our lives forever. You take it day by day, work hard, try your best, and keep a positive attitude—that's beautiful.

CHAPTER TWELVE

Rebuilding, Going Home

Lori:

My entire adult life, I've always been paranoid about unplugging things. When the kids were little, I would unplug their nightlights after they fell asleep. I unplugged blow dryers that were already turned off.

My dad had a house fire nine years ago and lost everything, including all of our childhood mementos and photos. When we finally got there, it was surreal. How could this have happened?

After the explosion, I felt like, "How could this happen to me again?"

I feel like we've overcome a lot of tragedy. My dad is a double amputee. He couldn't play ball with us and was an addict for years. My nephew was born with Goldenhar syndrome. And then my dad had the house fire, and then Kilee. You can never prepare yourself for anything. And you certainly cannot prepare for something like this.

To this day, I catch myself saying, "before the fire" and "after the fire." In some ways it has defined the chapters of our lives as a family. It was such a monumental moment in all of our lives and will continue to be because of how we now live as a result.

I don't want to dwell on the accident or allow it to define us forever. But everything is different now.

The biggest adjustment after moving into the new house was that we were still on the same land, so there were moments we still thought about the accident happening there. Even though we had a completely different floor plan with the new house, we were still in the same spot. But this was home, and our family was still together, and that's all that mattered to us.

Home was wherever my family was. And it was time to make new memories and create a new home for all of us.

Assessing Damage

In the beginning, we didn't think a lot about the house. There was so much going on with Kilee, and we wanted to make sure she was OK. Your mind just doesn't go to that place.

The day after Kilee was settled in at Shriners, we went to the house to talk to the insurance adjustor about the fire damage.

The adjustor walked in and walked right back out. He said, "It's a complete loss."

"Nothing? We can't save anything?"

When I finally did go into the house for the first time, it really was heartbreaking. Walking in, we felt like we had nothing left.

I was trying to be strong for the kids, and especially for Wade, because he couldn't go near his childhood home in ruins.

Boxes Held Our Lives

In June 2015, going through more than twenty boxes of "salvaged" items from our house was like, "OK, let's get this done and over with."

I was ticked.

So much was just trash. Broken, burned, and not salvageable.

It all smelled like fire. Not campfire. Campfire and house fire are not the same. House fire smell is horrible, awful. It was hard to look through the boxes. The smell took me back to that day on our neighbor's paved blacktop driveway, seeing Kilee and feeling the heat from our house as flames billowed out of Kilee's bedroom window.

Kilee's room, however, was burned the least of the entire house, so most of what Wade and I were sifting through in the boxes was her stuff, and she wanted none of it. None. She wanted a fresh start. And I really couldn't blame her. I felt the same way.

She's said this multiple times: "I've changed. Everything has changed. And my life is different now, and I'm OK with that."

I don't think she wanted the memories of it, and we didn't want the memories of it. Clothes that were saved smell like the chemicals used to get the smoke smell out, and I can't wear them. It's a reminder.

Construction Waiting Game

On November 28, 2014, we picked out the house we wanted to build, signed a contract, and paid our deposit.

It was still a ranch-style house, but we wanted a floor plan that was completely different than before so Kilee would never have to relive that day in her own home—how she came into the house and how she ran out of the house.

On December 26, we picked out everything else for the house: paint colors, floors, stonework, tiles, faucets, every little detail. I wanted to get everything done so we could move into our house as soon as possible. Our rental house's lease was up May 15.

The builder presented the house construction as "turn-key." They told us we would be in our home in ninety to 150 days. We had three friends who used the same builder, and it took them only ninety days to build their homes. It made us feel like we could get it done quickly and be in our home before our lease was up.

However, we kept getting told different things. Every time we met, something was wrong or delayed. Many things were not ordered on time and delayed the total construction by more than two months.

Where we were going to live was constantly on my mind. The old house was demolished on February 11.

Our original goal was to have the house torn down before Kilee was released from Shriners. But it didn't happen.

The morning after she came home, she had us walk her through the house. She wanted to see it. We asked if it bothered her that it was still there. And she said, "No, it's a reminder of what I've been through."

They didn't start digging until April.

I used to anxiously wait for the next day, the next vacation, the next big thing we had to do. But the construction of our house was different for me. I wanted it to be perfect for Kilee and for our family. I didn't want to rush anything. Everyone wanted the house to hurry up and get done. And I think we do that so much in life—getting excited about one day or one event. I don't want to feel like that. We have so much going on, so much in life to look forward to. Life is about every day.

We're here now, we're here as a family, and everyone is healthy and well.

I kept thinking that I didn't want to rush any construction. I didn't want anything to go wrong or have another accident. I didn't want anything bad to ever happen again.

Your mind goes there, for me, to stay calm. Two other homes I've had, I was very anxious. But this time, I was more like, "It is what it is. Let's be patient and content that we will get there someday soon."

The rental house didn't feel like home. Kilee didn't like living in that house. I think it was because it was across the street from where the old house was and where the new house was being built. The plus was we could keep an eye on the progress, watching contractors go in and out of the house.

For me, I was grateful to have a place to live.

And I reminded myself that it was all temporary.

After the rental house, we had to live in our camper for two weeks because the rental owners sold the house before we could move into our new home.

It was awful. Tight and cramped. Doogie, Digger, and our new puppy, Dori, wanted to run around and be dogs but couldn't. We had tiny closets, so we couldn't bring too many clothes. We didn't want to cook in such small quarters on a teeny gas stove, so we ate out a lot.

We were lucky to have it. It was an experience we'll never forget. We haven't stayed in our camper since.

Kilee:

We were having a rocky couple of weeks living in the camper with four people and three dogs. Taking showers and putting on lotion was awful in such a tight space.

Normally, my mom would sit on a stool to put lotion on me and put my garment sleeves on, but she had to stand up to do it in the camper because there wasn't enough room for a stool.

Once she got the lotion on, she had to put on my sleeves. They're tight anyway, and with the lotion, they get kind of slippery. She was standing in front of me and putting everything she had into pushing the sleeve up my arm with both hands. As she was trying to get the sleeves up, her hand slipped and punched me in the face.

I was shocked! I looked at her and said, "Oh my God, you punched me!"

She started laughing—a lot.

I was so stunned, I didn't know what to say. We both started laughing hysterically.

The Wait Is Over

Lori:

We finally moved into our new home in August 2015. It was surreal. It was like I didn't really process everything until I moved into the house.

We are on the same land where everything happened to Kilee. We've still got the pool out back as a reminder of when she ran out of the burning house and to the neighbors.

We bought clothes throughout the nine months we were without a permanent home, but we had not bought furniture or anything else. I started making lists of what we needed and had to buy before moving in, and it really put everything into perspective. We had lost everything.

I grieved that day. But we got through this, and now the kids have a place they can call home again. And it felt like home. But there are reminders; sometimes it's in the simplest things that we've lost.

Little things remind you of home, and now we look at it as our new home, our new life. We have memories from before, and they'll never go away. But now we're going to make new memories.

Things you have, those are items. Nothing can replace the love you have for your family. Leading up to moving into the house, those nine months, we'd been together that whole time. We're all OK and we are together, and that's what matters most. We are going to make it through. This is our new life, our new journey, all of us together. My house means family. When we walked into the new house, it was home. We were together, and we were home.

Kilee:

My favorite part of the house was my bedroom. I loved everything about it. It was a place I could go to get away from the rest of the family. It was one of the biggest bedrooms in the whole house, and I loved it. It was where I could have time to myself, where I could watch TV, where I kept all of my stuff, where I got dressed and ready every morning. It's where I could just be me.

When we moved into our new house, it felt good. Once we got all of our stuff in it, it felt like we were finally home. I think it felt that way for everyone because we knew we would finally be able to stay in one spot for a long time, instead of looking at everything as temporary. We had lived in the rental house and called it "home," but we didn't consider it home when we actually thought about it. I think the reason for us calling it home was because we believed that since all of our family was together, we were home. We knew that somehow we could then view it as more than a temporary home.

I was excited for my new room and my new everything, and I'm pretty sure the rest of our family was too. It feels great knowing we have a long-term home now. We had to live for so long without knowing where we were staying for the next few weeks because the house wasn't done yet. To know we don't have to do that anymore is great. We can now call it home and actually mean it.

I don't usually think about the house being in the same location as the old one. I know things happened there that I will always remember, but I never think about where I was. I think it's because the new house doesn't look anything like our old house.

Lori:

We stayed on the move the entire weekend that we moved into the house. In the middle of moving day, Kilee had a soccer game and I was keeping score as the assistant coach. No time to sit and relax.

It's a lot of work to move in general, but then I was also making sure Kilee was OK and Cameron was OK, and kind of Wade a little bit. He's pretty quiet about it. He hasn't said a whole lot. But I could tell he was getting more comfortable by that Sunday night.

You don't realize how much stuff you need when you've lost everything. I mean everything. When we moved into the new house, finally, we needed to buy everything—down to toilet paper, food and drinks, everything to stock a house for four people. It reminded me of moving for the first time and needing everything again.

That first night after we got everything moved in, it was weird for Wade and me. We thought the new floor plan would help make it feel OK that we were on the same land where the explosion happened. But it didn't help. That's etched into our minds. We know it happened there. We know Kilee ran out and to the neighbors after it exploded.

It didn't feel like home to me. It felt different.

Different, different, different.

We couldn't wait to cook supper in our new home. It didn't feel right at the rental house, and then Cameron was at a sporting event every night. Kilee was in therapy several times a week. Then we were delayed to get into the house several times, so we never knew when we should buy groceries. The house was "almost finished" for six weeks.

The second night in the new house, we made dinner and ate together as a family.

We had corn on the cob, baked macaroni and cheese—which is Kilee's and Cameron's favorite—and grilled chicken and steak. That's when it felt really good, sitting down together. It was nice.

Home is where our family is together, safe and sound, and we were glad to be home.

CHAPTER THIRTEEN

Senior Year

Kilee:

I needed to have senior pictures taken for the yearbook, and I had to wear a black drape.

I had to take off my shirt and just put the drape over my chest. It is a very uncomfortable thing to wear anyway because it is very awkward and feels like you don't have clothes on the upper part of your body. The drape comes very low on your shoulders and back, and I had never shown anyone my back. And yet, it was exposed for everyone in the gym to see while I waited to get my photo taken.

Before I changed, I had prepared myself for people looking and asking questions. When I came out of the locker room with my back exposed, I could tell that people were looking at it and probably wondering why it looked that way. I reminded myself that it didn't look nearly as bad as it had when it was blistered. Now it was just pink and splotchy—and kind of like patchwork.

While I was waiting for my turn, people were asking me questions.

"Why does your back look like that?"

"Is it normal for it to look like that?"

"Does it hurt?"

I didn't mind answering the questions because I knew people were curious and wanted to know. I felt comfortable answering them.

Lori:

The scars don't define Kilee, but they do define the way she lives her life. Her scars represent everything she stands for and will for the rest of her life.

She's not a victim of a house explosion. She survived a house explosion. To me, a victim is somebody who is faced with a challenge or tragedy but can't rise above it and make the best of his or her life. That's the complete opposite of Kilee.

We want everyone to realize that she survived this and she is living a normal life and achieving her dreams and goals. She's miraculous. She had the will to recover. She had the fight in her.

Graduating from Garments

Kilee:

My last Shriners appointment, in August 2015, went very well.

I was still wearing my garments. The nurses told me I didn't have to wear any kind of compression anymore, that I could use any type of lotion, and that I was basically finished with everything I used to have to do. It felt great to know I didn't have to do the things that were starting to consume my life. They told me I didn't have to go back to Shriners for a whole year, and that was the best news of all.

Knowing I was 90 percent finished with everything made me feel pretty close to back to normal. I loved knowing that, because I had missed the way things used to be: doing things on my own and not having to depend on my parents.

The typical time it takes to heal after burns is one year. And for some people, it is a little more than a year. The doctors told me I'd have to wear my garments for a year, but I got out of them early. And now I was finished with Shriners very early.

Each time I went back to Shriners, they were surprised at how well I was healing, and that would always make me feel hopeful. When they told me I'd reached the point that I didn't have to do anything special to make sure I would heal, I was surprised and very happy. I never thought that day would come, and when it did, it was almost hard to believe.

To be free of the garments meant so much to me. Plus, I was allowed to wear any kind of lotion. I have always loved wearing lotions that smell really good, so for me, that was exciting. It was another way for me to get back to normal.

ৡ৵৵

Lori:

We were in shock.

At Shriners, they always give you a paper to give to the scheduling desk when you leave. I saw that it said, "One year." I was thinking it meant Kilee would graduate from Shriners at the one-year mark. We were in month nine, and I figured we would go back in three months.

As we were leaving, I said to the lady at the security desk, "Bye! We don't have to see you for another three months!"

Kilee looked at me and said, "Mom, what's the matter with you?"

I said, "What do you mean?"

"Mom, I don't have to come back for ONE. WHOLE. YEAR!"

"No, it said, 'one year' on it."

"MOM, that's what that means. One year from now. One year from today I come back. I don't have to come back for a year!"

Her scars were "matured." She was finally at the finish mark, three months ahead of schedule. It was pretty awesome news.

Clean Slate

Kilee:

The first day of school for my senior year felt like any other. I woke up, got dressed and ready, ate breakfast, and left. I wore shorts and a simple shirt. The one thing that felt really different was that it was my last first day. I was a senior, and it still had not hit me. It was really strange to know I wouldn't ever have to go back to my high school at 8:00 AM and go to my classes, or see my friends in the hallways, or see my favorite teachers, or even sit in the chairs I had sat in for four years. I didn't like thinking about growing apart from my friends and so many of the people I enjoyed seeing throughout the day. My new beginning was another ending. In a way, I really didn't want to grow up.

I was a little nervous because I had so much to get done for college. But once I talked to my friends, I realized they all felt the same way.

I had a senior meeting with my guidance counselor, and she asked me where I wanted to go to college. I had no idea. She wanted to know what I wanted to do. I had no idea. I felt behind and unorganized; most of my classmates knew what they wanted to do. And I had no idea. But I know it's normal for some people to not know what they want to do, and I let it go. I figured I would sort it all out eventually.

Before, I wanted to be a veterinarian. But now, not so much. For one, I could never hurt an animal. To be a doctor, you have to take care of them by hurting them sometimes, like giving them shots. It's not really what I want to do anymore. My guidance counselor said she could see me as someone who works for a place as a spokesperson. Maybe for the Kilee Gives Back Foundation. Maybe...I don't know.

Senior year was a clean slate for me.

My junior year, there had been so many changes and ups and downs, then trying to catch up and get back on track. My senior year was different, and that felt really good. Not only did I have a clean slate, but so did everyone around me. No one had to worry about what to do or say around me. Things were like they used to be.

I was most excited about being able to get back to normal completely. It was the first year I was able to have the freedom I felt I needed. I could be with my friends and not have to worry about going to any therapy. I felt like my normal self, like I was able to do the things I used to do before the accident. I was finally finished with my recovery, which meant I physically felt like myself.

I was able to go back to playing soccer. That had been my ultimate goal ever since I started therapy. Being able to go back to soccer meant so much to me. I didn't think I would be able to at first, so when I realized I could actually do it, I felt really good about myself. I was able to play the whole season without having any issues, and I had a blast doing it. It was a bittersweet season because of it being my last year, but I knew I wasn't the only one who felt that way. My friends and I made the best of everything.

The year overall was good. I was very stressed about my college decision, especially because all of my friends already had chosen where they wanted to go and most of them knew what they wanted to do in life. I felt pressured to choose, but I enjoyed my senior year anyway. I had so much fun with my friends. We were able to do so many things together and completely experience the craziness of senior year together. We went to graduation parties together, we went to our senior dinner together, and we would go and eat after school together. Senior year was a very fun year!

But my senior year was still different from all of my friends'. No one else has a charity. And that's what I worked on when I wasn't in school or playing soccer. The foundation is something that's really important to me. I had more responsibilities than a typical seventeen-year-old. That's what prepared me to go to college, or for anything, really.

Junior year, at the beginning of the school year, I was like everyone else. I would go home after school and do nothing. I watched TV. But now, I'm doing what I want to help others have a better life—or at least that's my goal.

I know there's a reason why this happened to me. I think it has something to do with what I'm going to do with the rest of my life.

My relationships with my family have become a lot closer and better—even with my grandparents, whom I never saw a lot before, especially on my mom's side of the family. They never really made the effort. I didn't either, but

I think we're all making more of an effort now. Life is short. And people in my life have realized that you shouldn't let life bog you down or let things get in the way of what's important, and that is your family and the relationships you have with them.

Lori:

The temporary is gone: the chaotic therapy, the media whirlwind, the rental house, and the camper. When senior year started, Kilee was ready to start her new chapter. I told her, "Don't look back; keep moving forward."

In November of 2014, we were just taking baby steps. I would think about each day and how to get through it. I didn't think much about the future back then, but now I do so much more, because Kilee did overcome a lot and she continues to do really well.

In the hospital, I fell prey to what-ifs a couple of times. I worried about making sure she was comfortable with herself. We just kept giving her that confidence while she was there—everything happens for a reason. It's up to you to make meaning out of it. Afterward, she didn't want to go shopping or put makeup on—she didn't want to do anything. I wondered if she would ever get comfortable again. When she started doing her sports therapy in April 2016 and when she went to prom that year, it started kicking in for her again. And then vacation that year, she was starting to get back to herself. The number-one thing was when her hair grew back.

We just took it one day at a time, because we didn't know what she would or could do. We wanted Kilee to be comfortable with herself, above all.

So her senior year, I started feeling better as the school year went on, because Kilee didn't have garments on and she didn't have the restrictions she'd had. I started being able to take care of myself and not be stressed out about putting on the lotion, garments, stretching every night. I felt a little free from that. I didn't mind doing it, but it definitely did wear on me. I really appreciated the time I had to myself after that first year.

And I was really excited for Kilee. I cannot wait to see what she becomes. Everyone else was sad about the end of an era with their child in high school, but I was looking forward to what she will accomplish with her life and what she will continue to do with the good that came out of this tragedy. It's personal to her. I know she's going to do good things.

She graduated with honors, which is pretty remarkable considering everything she'd been through.

I've always told her and Cameron that in life, if you always try your best, you will find your way. It's like a stepladder: you're on your way up and you will get there. It just takes time.

Soccer Is My Escape

We were in one of Kilee's June appointments, before she graduated from Shriners, discussing her garments, when I asked what she was supposed to wear while she played soccer. It was too hot outside, and I wouldn't allow her to be over-heated and burn up trying to play while wearing garments. For one, it was embarrassing for her, and two, it was just too hot. With her progression of healing, I had to worry more about what she was comfortable wearing.

They let her out of the vest, sleeves, gloves, and a partial leg. They were going to allow alternatives to her garments since she was playing sports almost every day and going on vacations. They said whatever worked for us, give it a try. We put her in her garments at nighttime for about ten hours because she still had to be lotioned and massaged, and that greasy stuff gets all over the place. In the daytime, Kilee wore Spanx, because they were compression suits. And they worked. It was like night and day, literally, from wearing the garments. I don't know why it worked better for her, but it worked for Kilee.

We told her therapists how well the Spanx worked. We looked at the before photos of her buttocks, which aside from her arms were the worst burnt, and it was amazing. In two and a half months, it went from a blackish-purple, big, three-inch scar to flat and pinkish, like it's supposed to look. Even Kilee's nurses were impressed. And we were excited there was an alternative for kids who are recovering with scars and who want to play sports.

They were pleased with her playing soccer and keep-ing active, because with her doing throw-ins, it helped her stretch. Plus, Kilee's ankles, where she had grafts, got tight during the day, and the kicking and running helped keep them more flexible and limber. She can still feel her skin pull in, so you have to continuously stretch it back out, up to a year or sometimes longer, as long as she feels it.

Kilee:

I've been playing soccer since I was little.

I like it because it clears my mind. When I'm playing a game, I don't think about anything other than that game. You don't have to think about anything.

It makes me feel good knowing I'm out there on the field with my friends having a good time and playing a sport we all love. It's entertaining and fun. On the field, it feels like everyone is unstoppable, and that feeling is one of the greatest feelings ever.

My junior year's soccer season started off OK. I was excited because I could finally consider myself a veteran player and be a little more in charge—maybe get a captain spot.

It was an OK season, with plenty of ups and downs. But by the end of the season, I was considering not playing my senior year. But obviously, I was going to—it was my senior year. I wasn't going to skip out on it.

Fast-forward to the first night I played soccer since before everything happened, and I didn't feel nervous or scared at all. It felt like old times playing with my friends and having a good time. And I had been going to sports therapy since March, so I felt ready.

The first time I practiced soccer since the accident was on April 1, and the first time I shaved my legs, since my skin grafts and donor sites had healed, was twenty days later.

I wore no garments for the game, and it felt great to know I wasn't going to have to wear that stuff when I thought I would have to—it was hot. I thought I would have to wear my garments through the soccer season, and I knew that if I had to do that, I would be very uncomfortable. But since I didn't have to, I wore a sports bra, compression shorts, and my uniform. And for the first time since the explosion, my hair was long enough for a ponytail.

To put my hair in a ponytail for the first time felt good. I didn't like having short hair, and the way I knew it was growing was by putting it into a ponytail. I think it made me look more like me, too, because I had never had short hair; it had been hard for me to adjust to.

One of my friends always told me I should try putting it up into a ponytail. One day during practice, I finally let her try it, but I took it out because I wasn't sure if I liked it that much.

Then, the next week or so before practice, I bought a thick headband and wanted to try it out. I pulled my hair up and used the headband to hold back the stragglers. I actually loved it. It kept the hair out of my face when I was at practice and looked good too.

When I got to practice, all the girls told me they loved it. They all kept saying, "I told you so!" I was happy they thought it looked OK. I was excited I could finally start to get used to having hair to actually fix every day.

When I got home, I looked into the mirror and thought, *It kind of looks like normal me again.* It's a part of me that I didn't have for a long time.

When I walked onto the field for the first game, I got a little bit nervous, because I knew the people in the stands were watching and they were the people I went to school with. Everyone knew who I was, and I was scared I would be treated differently, even by my team. It was very nice of them to ask if I was all right, considering they knew how hard everything had been on me, but I wanted to be treated the same as everyone else. I wanted to go out there and play like I knew how to. And that is exactly what I did.

It didn't feel different to me at all. I had a blast, and I had been worried that I wouldn't, because I thought our team wouldn't be any good. It turned out I was wrong. We were actually really good, and everyone played well together. I never thought I could do this ever again, but I'm very proud of myself for being able to.

We won our opener 4-1. It felt great to know we'd had only a few practices with everyone there and we could still pull off a win like that. I couldn't wait to see what the season would hold for us! But I also wanted it to go slowly because it was my senior year; I didn't want this to ever end. Soccer always had been my favorite part of high school.

The greatest moment on the field my senior year was when I scored a goal against Eastern Brown High School. I felt the greatest I ever had in my high school soccer career.

Eastern had always been our rival. Their coach used to be our coach, and we had never beaten them. I really wanted to beat them. I knew we would all have to really try to win, and that is what we did. The whole game was back and forth.

It was 0-0, and we had only eight minutes left in the game.

There was a cross from the opposite side of the field that I was on, and I happened to be in the right place at the right time. I got the pass, and I shot the ball.

I shot and scored!

It was a very good goal, and I am happy with how it turned out. It felt amazing to know I scored the only goal in the game and helped win the game for us. I definitely was eager to score in this game.

Lori:

Her senior year, Kilee really regained her confidence. She was so humble through everything. She knew what happened, she accepted it, and she moved on. She was able to keep herself in the mindset that it was going to be OK when sometimes we would kind of drift off to, "What if it's not?"

She became an example for me, too, actually. There was an instance when she wanted to do something and I told her no. In the past, she would have pressed me on it. But this time, she didn't pursue it—she didn't push or pressure. She probably did that a lot to try to please me so as not to upset me.

Once the school year started, it was basically back to normal. She had the best soccer season she'd ever had. She was so proud of that. She had a lot of assists and multiple goals, and that was another confidence booster!

When I would see her doing something she loved, like soccer, it meant that much more to all of us, because she was striving again. She was doing something she wanted to do that she couldn't do for a while. It was a surreal feeling that, *Wow, she's going to be able to accomplish anything.*

One Year

Kilee:

November 10, 2015. The one-year anniversary of the explosion fell on the same date as my senior soccer banquet.

Mom was pretty emotional about it. I could tell that she felt proud of me.

I feel like the year anniversary was for both of us. I'm proud of her. She's always been there for me, and she's been through so much because of me. She's always helping, even though she's going through her own stuff.

Lori:

I made Kilee an album for her senior banquet, documenting the year with the entire family. I didn't want her to be really, really emotional. I felt like a way to do that was to show her how great our life is and how great our family is as a whole—trips, sports, dances, and giving back. It was something I could give her to show her what we all overcame with her together. The first year after the explosion taught us to live in the moment.

I still cry sometimes, and that's part of my process and how I'm healing. But I'm just grateful. Kilee was given a second chance. She is not a person who decided to give up. She's learned from all of this and wants to help others.

We were emotional that night, but we were all smiles. We were happy and grateful.

Big Sister...Again

Kilee:

Carter René Brookbank was born on February 8, 2016. The day before, I had talked to Brooke about how we had hoped she would go into labor when Cameron and I were with her and my dad. It was the day of the Super Bowl and we had plans to go to dinner for my dad's birthday. We went to dinner that night at one of my dad's favorite places, and the entire time I was trying to get Brooke to eat spicy foods, because I had heard that helps speed up labor.

After we got back home and a few minutes after we sat down to watch the Super Bowl, Brooke jumped up and looked at my dad and told him something didn't feel right. Her water had broken, and we went straight to the hospital. Carter was born the next morning.

This whole experience has been a major life changer for me. Throughout Brooke's pregnancy, I was so excited. I had always wanted a baby in the family and I never thought it would actually happen. I just couldn't wait to meet Carter, and it was such an exciting experience the whole time.

I knew I would love being a big sister because I already was one before, but it's different this time. This time I am a much older sister, meaning I can be there to help shape Carter into the person she will one day become. I already have seen so many amazing things from this little girl, and she's only a little more than a year old. I can't imagine what I will see from her in my lifetime.

With Cameron, I don't really remember much of him being a baby, because I was barely more than a baby myself. Now, with Carter, I am someone who will be there for her like a sister, and also be there as another role model in her life. I will be able to help raise her. The only bad thing is Carter and I will never be able to say we lived together. Because of our age difference, we can't do young-sibling things together.

Although some of these things are unfortunate, I am so excited to be able to be there for all of her life events. I will be like another parent to her at the same time as being her big sister. It is one of the best feelings ever knowing Carter is my little sister. I love coming home from college and seeing her. It makes visiting so much sweeter when she sees me and gets the biggest smile on her face. That makes up for being so far apart in age.

Over the summer after graduation, I was able to spend so much time with Carter, and that meant so much to me because I knew that would be the last time I was able to live with her completely. She was super young and I know she won't remember it, but I will always remember that I was able to see her grow and learn every day up until I left for college.

I had so much free time that I could spend all my time with Carter, and I loved every minute of it. Now, I am still able to see her grow up and change—it's just from a distance most of the time. Brooke and Dad both send me pictures and videos almost every day of Carter. I even get pictures from my mom and my Aunt Amy when they are all at work together. It is the highlight of my day to be able to get these adorable pictures of Carter showing off her personality. Sometimes I FaceTime her and talk for a few minutes, which is great every time.

When I go home and visit her, it always warms my heart, because when she sees me, she gets the biggest smile. It makes me so happy to know she knows who I am, because it was one of the things I was worried about leaving for college. Carter means so much to me. I have always loved babies, and having a real connection with Carter makes that love so much greater. Knowing I will always be her big sister and someone she will always be able to come to is a great feeling. I love her so much, and I love watching her grow up. Being a part of her childhood is so cool. I get to see her form into a little person so full of love and life, and it is the most incredible feeling.

Lori:

When I found out Jason and Brooke were having a baby, I was pretty excited myself! Kilee and Cameron had always wanted a little sibling, so that was pretty cool.

And I love having Carter to love on! Brooke works with me professionally, so Carter comes to the office three days a week, and she rules the roost. She knows everybody there loves and cares for her. We've thanked Brooke so many times for allowing us to be involved her life. It really is what I suspect is a grandma feeling: you're not really taking care of her, but you can spoil her.

We're proud of how we all get along and the family we've made. Divorce is hard for a lot of families to overcome, and maybe we wouldn't be this close if the accident hadn't happened. But it did bring us closer. Actually, a lot of good things came out of the accident.

Things happen in your life that cause you to make decisions you wouldn't have made otherwise. And that can be a very good thing.

We genuinely love Brooke and Carter. They're a huge part of our life. We're looking forward to Carter growing up. We talk about her playing sports and what it'll be like to see her in high school.

When Brooke had Carter, I was at the hospital with everyone. We started getting an even stronger relationship from there. And she's wonderful to my children. How could you not love someone who's wonderful to your kids? She's the sweetest, nicest person you could ever meet.

And Kilee is an amazing big sister. She's going to be a remarkable mother someday. It shows in how she feels about

Carter and how she treats her. She wants to take care of her. It's a very comforting feeling to know how loving and caring she is.

The Big Decision

Kilee:

Making a college decision was by far one of the most difficult things for me to do. Even figuring out which schools to apply to was a tough part of the whole process. I originally wanted to be far from home, somewhere like New York City. After I realized just how far away I would be, I realized it just wasn't something for me. I decided I should probably be somewhere a little closer to home because of my new little sister and the rest of my family. I wanted to be a part of Carter's life, and I felt that if I went far away from home, I would never be able to see her. I feared she simply wouldn't know who I was when I did come back to visit.

After getting accepted to three of the six colleges I applied to, I still procrastinated on deciding—big time. (I'm not one who gets things done early!) My three options were the University of Cincinnati, Xavier University, or Miami University. I had no idea what to do.

I didn't want people to think that the only reason I went to Xavier was because of my cousin, Loren, who's a year ahead of me in school. But after a lot of thought and realizing that it was the best option for me, I decided I would attend Xavier. Of course, I had to make sure Loren was OK with me choosing the same college, and she was. She was excited to hear I would be joining her, and she had no problem with it at all.

Looking back on my choice now, I wouldn't change a thing. I love Xavier and all the connections and relationships I have made since starting school. I am close enough to home that I can visit whenever I want to, and I am far enough away that I can have a sense of freedom. I am so happy I decided to go to Xavier. Loren and I are back to the way it used to be in high school, but even better. We are so close and see each other every day. We eat lunch together, and any time one of us is bored, we just ask if the other wants to hang out. It's so nice having her around all the time.

When the time came and I was graduating high school, I never thought I would be able to graduate with honors. Before the accident, I had plans of graduating with honors and going above and beyond, but when I was in the hospital, I thought it was impossible. My teachers helped me because they knew my situation, which is probably the only reason I got through it. I had to catch up on so much that I felt like I should just give up and take whatever grade I got.

My teachers are the ones who motivated me to do things. They knew I had a rare situation and that, at times, I physically couldn't do my work. Because they understood this, they made things so much easier on me. Right after I got out of Shriners, all of my motivation was lost. I did not want to do anything but rest, even though I knew that wasn't an option.

Graduating with honors was something I had always wanted to do, just to be able to say that I did it. The fact that I was able to graduate with honors despite everything that was going on in my life makes me feel that much better about it.

Lori:

When Kilee picked Xavier, I felt amazing! I thought, *This is awesome!* I had been excited to see what steps these kids are going to take for a very long time. You try to give them the tools to make the right decisions, and when it's time to go to college, you have to have your stuff in order.

I knew I would be missing her, I knew I'd be upset, but I was ecstatic and excited for her decision. I loved that she would be staying close to home and be able to see her brother and her baby sister.

I was a little disappointed she didn't get into all the schools where she applied, but again, I knew it must have happened for a reason. She didn't need to be that far from home. But if she'd gotten in, I'd have supported her 100 percent.

She'd always wondered if she'd really be able to go if she got in somewhere eight to twelve hours away. So with the way things worked out, she didn't have to make that hard decision.

Senior Prom

Kilee:

As senior year came to its end, it was time for prom again in the spring, and once again, this dance had its own twist to it: *Inside Edition* wanted to do a story on me to run on national television.

I was shocked. I was amazed that a big TV show like that would want to do something about me. At the same time, I was also very hesitant. I knew I had already done something like this for my last prom, and it turned out to be a big disaster that I was not happy about. My mom kept reassuring me it wouldn't be like that this time and that we would set some ground rules for them once they got there. After hearing this, I was still a little hesitant, but leaning in the right direction.

Once my mom told me they would bring professional hair and makeup artists, that was it for me. I knew I had to do it, because the one time I had ever had my hair and makeup professionally done, I was on *The Doctors*, and it was an incredible experience. They were great at what they did and made me look great, so I knew if I had the opportunity to have that again, I should take it.

The day started off with the camera crew interviewing me. They were super nice and made it so easy to talk about things. After that was getting my hair and makeup done. I showed each of the ladies what I wanted, and both of them delivered. I felt like a Kardashian on reality television, like a real celebrity who got her hair and makeup done every day—I wish! A girl can dream, right?

I was so pleased with how it all turned out, and when I finally got to put my dress on, my day got even better. My dress was beautiful, and I still love it to this day. It matched my hair and makeup perfectly. There was only one downfall of the whole night, and that was when the *Inside Edition* crew said they needed to be in the actual dance. This was something I was unaware of and was not happy with. Looking back, I understand why they had to be in there. I was on prom court nominated for queen. Apparently, some-one told them that I had won, so they wanted to get footage of that happening. I threw a fit about them being there because they wanted to follow me around the whole time and sit by me and my group of friends. That was just annoying to me. They agreed to keep their distance, and I agreed to let them stay.

I won prom queen, which was exciting, but it's not something girls should swoon over the way they do. My life continued the same way it always had after that night.

Overall, I had a great night. I was in a party bus with my best friends. We all went and ate dinner, which ended up being paid for by a Cincinnati Bengals player who came into the restaurant, and then we went back to the school for the dance. Some of us even met up afterward to hang out some more. It was a very fun night.

CHAPTER 14

The Next Phase

Kilee:

In May 2016, before high school graduation, Mom and I released the first edition of *Beautiful Scars*. We had our launch event at Shriners in Cincinnati, and I was interviewed by local TV a few more times.

To say I am a published author sounds so sophisticated and like it comes with a celebrity life. I always felt like my life would soon become like Dan Humphrey's in *Gossip Girl,* living on the Upper East Side of New York City and being able to afford it. That is so not the case! My life has stayed completely the same. The only thing that has changed is that I now have a very dramatic "fun" fact to tell people while we are doing our icebreakers to get to know our classmates better!

A few weeks later, on June 2, I finally turned eighteen, and it felt great! It was the sense of freedom that every teenager longs for since they were sixteen years old. Even though I was still living at home with my parents, I was given so much more freedom. Of course, I had to beg for my curfew to be later, but I was able to do so much more than I was able to do before. My parents knew I was always a responsible person, so they knew I would be responsible with the freedom they gave me.

Sharing the Message

Over my summer break, we made time to travel and speak to people about what I have been through. I went to hospitals, Shriners meetings, libraries, and so much more. I love being able to tell my story, because it is one that people often find inspiring. Most people want to hear about it and learn more about Shriners; that is one of the reasons why I love speaking to people. I love teaching people who otherwise might not have known about Shriners. It is very rewarding knowing I am helping Shriners in some way.

While that is a great feeling, my favorite thing to do is to interact with the patients at Shriners. I love talking with them and hearing their stories. I know that most children are emotionally damaged from what they have been through, and I am perfectly OK with sharing my story with them. I hope to inspire them to want to keep getting better and to keep trying harder. And if it is possible, I want them to be OK with sharing their story, too. I love being able to help people, and that is what I hope I am doing when I speak to different groups.

The most memorable reaction I have had after speaking is when I visited the Shriners hospital in Boston in August 2016. I was able to meet with a little girl and her parents. She was about seven years old and had been badly burned. She was in the miserable phase of her hospital stay, the part I thankfully don't remember much of from my own recovery. I got to talk with this little girl and tell her that at one point, I was just like her. I showed her how I looked and reminded her that she could look just as good as I did with my scars. I encouraged her to keep fighting. I'm not sure if I made her feel better, but I know for sure that I made her parents feel better. They were able to realize how far I had come, and they knew their little girl could do the same.

It was so memorable because it was the first time I was ever able to talk to a current patient. I had talked to patients like me who went back to the hospital occasionally, but that was the first time I was able to reassure a family that their child would be OK and still live a normal life.

Meeting other people like me always makes me feel like I am a part of a community. We all have been through our own struggles, and we are able to bond over them. I have made lots of new friends because of my summer travels and adventures to places like Boston, Las Vegas, and Sacramento, as well as local events in the Cincinnati area. It is so much fun being able to connect with others on a level that most adults wouldn't even understand.

ৡ৵৶

Lori:

I see her standing in front of large groups of people and talking, and I think, *Is this my child? There's no way this is my kid!* I knew she was confident, but I didn't know she was that confident to be capable of doing things like that. After the fourth or fifth time I saw her being interviewed, I was like, *Yeah, she'll nail this.*

She speaks from her heart. She doesn't prepare a lot, because she speaks what's on her mind, and it's very real. She doesn't use notes or anything; it's very natural. I am highly impressed.

There is a whole other level of Kilee that we hadn't seen before. Probably almost every time she speaks in public, I get a little tear in my eye. I always say, "She's just special. She has a mission."

When Kilee speaks, it's not planned out. That's what's great about Kilee. She's not trying to get everyone's approval. It's from her heart. Her intentions are in the right place.

College: A New Adventure

When it was time to take Kilee to Xavier, I was excited for the drop-off day, but a little anxious. I just wanted it to be over so I didn't have to keep worrying about it. Loren being there made it much easier, because I knew if Kilee needed somebody, Loren would be there for her.

That day, Kilee drove herself. I rode with Wade, and Brooke and Jason rode together. It was a little weird in the morning to realize we were going to drop Kilee off and she wouldn't be back for at least a month. I knew the emotions would come later, but I just wanted to get through the day. When we were on campus, they kept us busy. We got to meet the roommates and their parents, and we felt really good about that.

Kilee's room was small. So I tried not to focus on her being gone from me. Instead, I focused on complaining about the size of the room, just to take my mind off the bigger picture.

We helped her put her stuff away, get organized, and make her bed. It was a really neat experience, because we were there to help her go on her next step.

As part of the day, they take you into the gym and give you an hour-long lesson on leaving your kids. We were in an assembly with the president and dean of students. At one point, they said, "OK, hug your loved ones now." They talked about how important it is that parents "be there" for their kids but not be actually there. In the middle of all of this, Kilee and I started cracking up. Something got us laughing and we couldn't stop, and that helped us get through without crying. We found humor instead of sadness. We were being strong and not getting too upset about the change.

When we walked out, we told Wade about it, which was another five minutes of getting a chuckle.

After the assembly, the parents were asked to leave. I didn't cry and Kilee didn't cry. We needed that laugh.

She's not going away forever, I thought, *it's only an hour away.* If she needs to come home, she can, and if we need to see her, we can. When we walked out the door, we said our goodbyes, gave her a hug, and she was fine.

The students have a very busy, structured first three days of orientation. I looked forward to getting the calls from Kilee every night. The first night, she told me she'd met somebody and he was so cute. I felt better that she'd made friends. I guess part of me was worried about people staring, but we expect it, so we ignore it. I don't pay that much attention to it anymore; I know in my heart she'll be fine.

Kilee:

Coming to a whole new place, I knew it would be tough making new friends. I have never been great at making friends. I was worried about living with someone I didn't know, and I was worried about making connections with new people. I had always heard people say that the friends you make in college last forever.

Surprisingly, only a handful of people asked me about my scars, and they were people I was familiar with. I was comfortable sharing with them, and I think the only reason they didn't ask sooner was because they were worried I would be offended. At Xavier, I feel completely comfortable and accepted. I love Xavier, and I am happy to know I'll be there for the next few years.

Having a roommate is something every college freshman is unsure about at first. It is hard to imagine yourself living with someone you don't know at all. And to be completely honest, it is a strange thing to get used to. Once you adjust and understand that almost everyone has to do it, it isn't so bad. I enjoy living with someone who is very similar to me, and I have become friends with my roommate.

There's actually a crazy story that goes along with this. My roommate is from Chicago, and her best friend from high school goes to Xavier too. When we were first getting to know each other, she had asked if I knew someone named Joanne. This caught me off guard, because Joanne was my nurse at Shriners. My roommate's friend and her family are friends with Joanne and her family. They lived right beside each other! I thought that was so cool and just proved that we actually live in a very small world, and you never know how you are going to make connections with people.

Most people look back on high school and think about how much they wish they were in high school still. I don't feel that way. High school was a great time in my life, but now that I know what college is like, I would never want to go back. College life is extremely fun, and the freedom I have now is something I would never give up. I love college, and the new friends I have made here are a big part of the reason I enjoy it so much.

But I do miss my high school friends an incredible amount. I think it would be cool to be able to experience college with the people you spent your whole life with in high school and grade school. I miss having our gossip sessions whenever we needed it, I miss playing soccer with them, I miss hanging out with them, and I just miss them being around.

I'm very happy, though, that I've moved on from some relationships and that I've learned from them. I am a strong believer that certain people are in certain periods of your life for a reason. Some are part of a learning process, and some are there to stay. Either way, you are supposed to learn from these people. People change, feelings change, and relationships change. It is all a part of life, and everyone will experience it at some point. In the past few years, I have learned a lot about myself and the people around me, and I'm a better person for it.

Lori:

Kilee had been gone about three months, when the second anniversary of the accident was approaching.

She didn't know if she'd be able to do anything on November 10, so I'd messaged her friend earlier that week and told him I really wanted to surprise Kilee on the two-year anniversary. I couldn't imagine going that day without seeing her. I wanted to just go and surprise her at the dorm. So he told her he would take her to dinner, and we stood outside and waited for them. When she came down, she was stunned! She was so excited!

I felt so much better about it, being able to see her. I wouldn't have been able to forgive myself if I'd known I could have gone and didn't.

I made sure I told her I couldn't imagine not seeing her on that day. It's just more of a memorial type of thing. We know what happened, and we know where we are today as a result. And we feel like we're better people because of it.

Something happens every single day that makes me think about the accident or get a little emotional. For a while, probably until Kilee went to college, I still cried every day. When she left, I was able to let go a little bit. She's an adult, and she's able to be more responsible for herself.

I can't always take care of Kilee 24/7, and it's not my job anymore. She's a young woman, and she's living her dreams, and I accept that.

I started missing her around the anniversary and close to the holidays. I got really emotional at that time. I started to see, too, how much of an impact she'd had on Cam and how much she affected him when she was home. We made it a joke: "She doesn't need to stay at college. She can just come home." She gets a kick out of that but says, "Mom, I'm never coming back to the country!"

When she came home for Thanksgiving, it really hit me. We'd also gone to Las Vegas with her earlier that month for a Shriners golf event and spent extra time with her around the anniversary, and we had a book signing in November, too. Getting back in the habit of seeing her made it hard to get used to not seeing her again.

An Unexpected Romance

Kilee:

I am in a new relationship now, and it has been one of the best experiences of my life. We met at Xavier, and it all is actually a crazy story. We were in the same orientation group and immediately connected. After orientation weekend, we realized that we lived in the same building, on the same floor. We ended up being in the same first-year class that every freshman has to take. Everything was perfectly aligned for us to meet each other.

Thinking about that now, it is really a crazy thing, and I love telling the story. Because we didn't know each other before college, it is so much fun to get to learn new things about each other. The first time I told Alec about my story, we had known each other for only a couple weeks. We had been spending a lot of time together, and I felt like he had wondered about it for a while. I didn't want to not address the elephant in the room, so one night when we were just talking and getting to know each other, I told him everything. Telling someone who didn't already know me about my story was something I had done multiple times before. But this time was different. I knew I wasn't telling someone I would probably never see again. I was telling a person I knew would be around, and somehow I wasn't nervous.

He reacted so well to it and continued to be the same person toward me. He didn't change the way he felt, and that meant so much to me. Of course, he still had a lot of questions, but I let him know I was OK with talking about it and that he could always ask anything if he was curious.

Forming a new relationship with someone wasn't as hard as I originally thought it would be. It wasn't something that was planned; it just happened. I think that is what is so cool about it all. I didn't come to college looking for someone, because I was just out of a relationship. I came to college with the mind-set that I was going to do my own thing, and if something happened to come along, I would consider it.

Once I had been around Alec for a little while, I was hoping that something would come of us meeting. Like I said before, relationships are meant for certain parts of your life; some are going to last, and some aren't. I was happy to move on with my relationships, and I still am so happy that I was fortunate enough to realize all of this.

Lori:

At first I thought, *Oh, great, she's met friends.*

Then I thought, *Take it easy and get to know each other. You'll know if it's right to be together.*

At first, they just hung out with their group of friends. Kilee was smitten, but it didn't really get serious until October. They're really close as friends, too. They got personal before getting together as a couple.

As a mom, you're always going to worry about other people loving and accepting your child. I thought, *Wow, if he's accepting of her scars and all she's been through, then he must be a remarkable kid.*

Looking to the Future

Kilee:

I am looking forward to where I will go next. Before college, it was the furthest I could see into the future. Now I realize after college I can go wherever I want and do whatever I want. I don't have to go back home to my parents; I will be old enough to live life on my own.

I am excited and nervous at the same time for this, because it is always scary to not know what will happen, but that is also the fun part. I get to make my life how I want it and learn more about myself along the way. For now, I will just continue to live my life one day at a time.

CHAPTER FIFTEEN
In My Own Skin

Kilee:

I am not the same girl who was in that fire three years ago. I have changed into a whole new person with each and every one of my experiences. From high school, to the fire, to the hospital, to writing a book, to college, I have grown into the person I am today. I have always been mature for my age, and I would say that is still true. I still have pieces of who I used to be, and they always will be part of me. But with every new experience, change comes in us all.

I hope that with every experience I encounter, I learn and grow from it. I am most proud of myself and how I can come to terms with what I've been through and not dwell on how my life used to be. I could think about how my life is so different, and how I wish things would go back to the way they used to be, but I don't do that. I choose to take a different approach and learn to live with the fact that things happen and there is nothing we can do about them but let life go on.

I am a genuine person. Everything I say, I mean. When people think of me, I want them to think that I'm a good person, because that is what we are all trying to be—good people. I can only hope to continue growing into the new and different parts of my life to be the best person I can be.

My scars don't define me. But they have given me a new life. A different life. A life worth living. I'm defined by my actions and how I started to live despite my scars.

I'm defined by how I treat others. And I'm defined by my courage. They are my beautiful scars, but they aren't only my badge of honor—they're only a piece of me. I define me.

My scars define how I live.

They changed the way I do things and how I look at things and the way I feel, but they're not who I am. They're just another part of me.

I noticed that my scars are fine the way they are. They were very tough to get moving at first, but I knew eventually they would get better. I grew to love them and accept them. Especially since I knew they would always be there. I noticed that no one really cared about seeing them and that the people who did care didn't matter to me.

My scars represent me and who I am and who I have become. They represent what I have been through. I see strength and a story. I would like to think other people think the same things when they see them. To me, my scars mean that I am strong and can get through anything. I know myself and my story, and how I got to where I am now. I will always be proud of myself when I look at my scars.

I don't think people look at me differently, and if they do, it's because they know more about my personality and how I am. I can tell my friends are the same toward me. When people look at me, I want them to know my story and know that they, too, can get through anything.

I have scars inside as well. The emotional scars are sometimes more painful than the scars people can see; they are the ones no one knows about. Most people don't know what I have been through, but I do. These kinds of scars are just as beautiful because they tell me I can get through anything.

Strong as Steel

Lori:

In the beginning, I thought, *What will people think? She's so beautiful, but what will people think when they see her scars? What will they do, look at them or stare?*

We learned a long time ago not to be offended by stares.

Kilee's scars are beautiful. They show her fight and what she's been through and what she's been able to achieve and overcome: learning to walk again, feed herself, use the bathroom on her own.

Honestly, when I look at her, I don't even notice the scars anymore. They don't identify who she is. They show what she's been through. I think for Kilee to walk around and not worry about it is awesome. She lives freely and doesn't stress about some scars on her body.

I know myself, and I'm not as strong as her. I know I would have long-sleeved mesh on or something so you wouldn't see anything. I have stretch marks on my stomach, and even though I'm skinny, I'd never dare wear a bikini where other people would see me. I'm super impressed by Kilee's strength.

Just knowing she's alive cancels out any scarring on her body. I don't even get sad about her scars, and she's the same way. She doesn't care.

She says to me: "I'm here. I'm alive. I have a purpose to serve. I need to figure out what it is."

She's not finished, and she's got a lot more to do in her life.

I'm watching her become this incredible person, and I'm in awe of her continued growth. She wants to help people realize their stories, their purposes, and then live that. She wants to see people make their dreams reality, turning any obstacles into what thrusts them into a life worth living. Kilee is looking forward to the future. It's a new chapter. This is the beginning of her life as an adult.

Kilee is self-sufficient and comfortable on her own. Our relationship is close, but we don't have to see each other constantly to be that close. We talk every day. We text "I love you" and "goodnight."

Kilee is, hands down, one of the strongest people I know—especially after everything she's been through. She has always been able to look at life with the attitude: "I'm here now."

I've always been super close with her. She knows she can talk to me about anything and I'm not going to judge her (though I may discipline her or correct her).

Our bond doesn't go away. No matter where we are, we will still talk every day. It's special.

When the explosion first happened, Kilee wanted her dad. She's never wanted her dad. She's always wanted me. I've always been with the children. He worked, and I took them to work with me. I've seen them almost every day of their lives. It was odd that she wanted Jason. It was like she knew who could handle it and be strong for her. And at that time, it wasn't me. She knew her dad would be stronger. It was an instinct she had.

Before the accident, she talked to him about nothing, and now since the accident, she opens up to him. He's a great dad. I think the bond she and I have will never go away, but I'm glad she reached out to him when all of this happened.

It's gone beyond what most parents will ever experience with their child. Her scars don't define her, but they've helped make her who she is and define how she handles situations. And her scars certainly have made me who I am, just in trying to be a better mom and a better person overall.

Watching her overcome all the obstacles made me realize you truly can get through anything if you put your mind to it and have a great support system. My new motto became #grateful.

I've told her, don't limit yourself in what you want to achieve in life or who you want to be with. Just take your time and learn.

People always say to me, "It's sad…" And I do cry sometimes still, but when I see her scars, I see life.

Because of her scars, I was able to watch her at her homecomings and prom. I was able to watch her graduate, to help her pick a college, and watch her journey. And someday, I'll be able to watch her get married and start a family of her own. This is all because of her beautiful scars.

I feel absolutely blessed that she's still here with us. Every time I look at Kilee, her nineteen years of life flash through my mind. All of the memories are crystal clear.

The one thing about the accident is that she'll never forget. Her beautiful scars came from that. She has recovered from every aspect. It's a daily reminder for her to look at herself and think, *I'm alive. I'm here.* And I'm grateful, because that's how I view them.

People look at her and just see her smile and how pretty she is, and it takes away from all the painful days, the ugly days that we fought back to get through to get to the other side. She is pretty. But her beauty and strength go much deeper than her smile. Her scars remind her of the spirit and fight she has behind her smile.

CONCLUSION

Kilee:

I don't let what happened stop me from thinking about the future, because anything could happen, anytime. You can't live your life worried about what could happen and when. If something happens, it's going to happen. What are you going to do about it?

When people hear my name, I want them to think I am someone like them. I want them to know they can do anything. I want them to be inspired.

I want them to think, *She got through it; so can I.*

Before the explosion, I was into normal teenage things. I didn't think about life or how easily something could happen to me or my friends or anyone, really. Now, I worry about things that matter in my life. I think about what I'm going to do with my life and my family.

Even though this is the biggest challenge of my life, I plan to make the best of it. I want to inspire others who are like me, or who are in any way similar, and just need someone to talk to, to help them through rough times. I have had some very kind things said about me, and I want to pass all of that love and support along to others.

Lori:

I'm so proud of the way Kilee has been able to overcome everything and be a positive influence on others, especially children. Kilee wants them to realize that your image is so much deeper than scars on your arms. It's an unbelievable feeling to know, *Wow, that's my daughter.*

And I'm certainly not taking all the credit. Jason's been a good dad, always.

People always say, "I don't know how I'll make it through this." For me, I'm proud that I have stayed positive through this. So quickly you can turn and start having negative feelings and thoughts. Something huge in our lives is the concept of, "Be the bigger person." You're going to make mistakes, but be the bigger person.

We've done good things out of this situation. We wouldn't have the publishing company, KiCam Projects, and the foundation if not for all of this. And our family has come together: Amy, Jason, Brooke, all of us. We have such a special bond with our friends; we know who our true friends are. My stepdad, Jay, was there the first day Kilee walked again. Those memories will never go away, and we're grateful forever for it. I don't want to ever be bitter about anything.

I get so excited to think about what Kilee and Cameron are going to accomplish. Both kids are highly intelligent. They're both excited about doing the charity work. They both really want to help people and give back. I can't wait to watch them continue to grow and have careers and families of their own. Will they be involved in the family businesses? Which college will Cameron pick? Will Kilee get a master's, and where will she go?

I'm not sure what Kilee's future will hold exactly, but I have a feeling it'll be something with communications. I think she'll be doing something that involves speaking and presenting. She enjoys that, and she's good at it. I definitely think she has a career in helping people.

I always tell both kids, "Don't ever limit yourself. You can do anything you put your mind to, and if your heart's not in it 100 percent, don't do it."

Who Is Kilee Brookbank?

Kilee:

I am a person filled with strength and love. Someone who has passion for what she does. Someone who cares about people and things and doesn't let anything else get in the way of that. Those are the things I want connected to my name. I want other people to think of me as all of those things.

I want people to think of me as someone they can look up to, especially my brother and my baby sister.

I want to pass along any big-sister wisdom that I can. I'm excited to be there for my siblings. I want them to know I'm there for them no matter what they need.

When Carter is old enough to understand, I want to tell her everything that I've been through. I would explain to her that whole day—everything that happened. I would make sure I tell her in a way that would inspire her to never give up on anything, no matter what she might be going through. I want to be the person she can come to for advice about anything in her life. I think I could really help her, especially if she knows what I've been through and overcome. I would definitely tell her that it might seem like there isn't anything more to life than what goes on in school or with her friends, but eventually something will happen that will show her there is more to life than the small things. There certainly is for me.

I am very grateful that I have this life. I wouldn't trade it for anything in the world.

ACKNOWLEDGMENTS

We would like to thank all of our friends, family, and community for their love and continued support over the past year, as well as Shriners Hospitals for Children-Cincinnati, WCPO.com, Ripley DECA, the Cincinnati Reds, Emmy Jenkins Photography, Justin Bieber, *The Doctors*, and SB Projects, as well as everyone at Ripley-Union-Lewis-Huntington and Georgetown Junior/Senior high schools.

We also are grateful to everyone who has been involved with the Kilee Gives Back Foundation and the Kilee Brookbank Celebrity Golf Tournament. (You can learn more at KileeGivesBack.org.)

We could not have come so far without you, and we are committed to paying forward all that we have been given.

With love,
The Brookbank and Highlander families